OH CALIFORNIA

Oh California, I came to you when I was young
you are a state of mind, your praises I have sung!
You are known throughout the world as our Golden State
even one of your bridges is called "The Golden Gate."
Junipero Serra built the missions for it was his duty
doing God's work and seeing much of your natural beauty.
You are 800 miles long and offer us so much variety
the beaches, the mountains or desert; oh what diversity!
From San Diego, Crescent City, Death Valley to San Francisco
Oh California, we are even proud of your famous sourdough.
You stand so strong and tall among our United States
30 million of us enjoying your many beaches, rivers and lakes.
The earthquakes awaken us to enjoy you day by day
be it Tahoe, Shasta, Yosemite or a sunset by the bay.
Places like The Mother Lode, The Redwoods or your famous coastline
is rich in history and the view is one of a kind
No matter where I visit, I know that I'm not alone
for the brown bear flag lets me know that I'm home!
Oh California, I am getting older and someday I will die
but I'll be happy knowing I'm buried under the California sky

By Michele Marie McCarthy ©1991

John Hamilton

KGO Radio Talk Show Host

This book is the accomplishment of KGO Radio listeners - mostly those who listen Saturday mornings to John Hamilton *On The Go With KGO.* I thank each one of you who contributed a story. You really make a difference.

Money from your purchase of this book goes to the Bay Area Big Brothers/Big Sisters organization, which offers children a helping hand in life. This book also offers another opportunity for KGO Radio listeners to get to know KGO Radio listeners. I bet you didn't know there were so many talented "On The Goers" like yourself?

This project, without the time, talent, and resources of many people, would still only be an idea. Their names are listed in the book.

To Barnes and Noble, thanks for featuring "**On The Go**" in your stores around Northern California.

One of my favorite places to go in Northern California is KGO's Studio A on Saturday mornings. That's where I broadcast *On The Go With KGO.* From 5 a.m. to 8 a.m., I talk with listeners and guests about travel and outdoor

John and listeners on the Salty Lady.

topics. Not only do we have fun together, but we learn from each other.

It was a listener and old friend, the late Chapman Wentworth, who pointed me in the direction of La

Porte and the Lost Sierra. This place offers a glimpse of "old" California, brimming with colorful stories of the settlers, the Gold Rush and skiing. Skiing? Yes, it was Northern California where the first organized ski races took place in North America. Scandinavian gold miners raced their long "skis" on snowy Sundays with bets flowing like their homemade kickapoo joy juice. Another listener talked about the incredible view from the highest point in the continental United States – Mount Whitney. A huge cloud obscured the scenery on the Father's Day that I climbed over the rocks to the summit. It didn't matter. More peak experiences followed on Mount Lassen and Mount Shasta. Then there's Bob Fuel, the proprietor of the "North

Coast of California" and its "capital," Honeydew. I think every KGO employee has a Honeydew hat, shirt or button.

From "On The Goers" we have learned about fall colors around Quincy in Plumas County, and on the eastern slope of the Sierra; about sipping tea at Brambles in the Central Coast town of Cambria; and camping in the sand dunes of Pismo Beach. I've been Gulliver in the pygmy forest near Mendocino; a trader on the Pomo Indian trading trail above Jenner; a rafter on the Klamath, Russian, and American rivers. I love whale watching with 42 KGO listeners every Memorial Day. We contribute to the KGO Leukemia Cure-a-thon to sail to the Farallons with Salty Lady skipper Roger Thomas, who has contributed so much over the years to KGO's major charity.

Blessed we must be. Northern California is the land of majestic mountain peaks, deep, fertile valleys, great open plains, lush forests, long sandy beaches, and great bays and ocean. We have raging white water rapids and delicate wildflowers that paint California's landscape ten months of the year. It is a wonderful place.

The intent of this book is to inspire us all to experience the vast natural riches of Northern California. That, after all, is one of the purposes of John Hamilton *On The Go With KGO* every Saturday morning.

Top: John at the summit of Mt. Shasta.
Middle: Cooling off with mountain biking friends during a ride on Mt. Shasta.
Bottom: John checking out geology in high-Yosemite country.

Inside ON THE GO...

Oh California (The Poem) 1

John Hamilton Letter 2

The Forward 5

Big Brothers/Big Sisters 6

KGO Personalities 8

North Coast Region 22

Gold Country 34

Shasta Cascade Region 38

High Sierra Region 44

Central Coast Region 48

The Bay Area 52

Beaches 84

SafetyTips When Traveling 88

Bed & Breakfast Inns 90

Highlights 92

Top Things To Do 100

Index 110

Calendar of Events 112

More about ON THE GO...

Copyright ©1995 by Entertainment Direct

ISBN 0-9648114-0-5.

Publisher
Entertainment Direct
2530 Berryessa Rd.
Suite 212
San Jose, CA 95132
408-441-2050

Art Director
John Panetta

Photographers
Faye Dawdy
Verne Paule
Diana Petersen

Story Editors
Debi Barker
Kathleen Cha
Allison Hodges
Richard Nelson
Anne Panetta

Layout
Mark Bonasera

Pre-press
Argyle Imaging

Printed By
Aaccurate Printing

The Forward

John E. Panetta, Entertainment Direct

"On The Go With KGO Radio" was a pleasure to produce. It was a joy to work with Barnes & Noble Bookstores for allowing us to showcase the book in their stores, the Big Brothers/Big Sisters organization, the photographers and story editors, all the KGO Radio personnel who helped make it possible, and especially all the many listeners, because without your help and participation—this book would be only an idea.

All the places and things described in the book come directly from KGO Radio's many listeners, on-air personalities, and other special people. I enjoyed the fact that Gov. Pete Wilson submitted his favorite place to go (see page 78), and in a non-election year, too!

The folks who submitted ideas and photos are to be commended. Because you submitted your words and photos and allowed us to reproduce them with no strings attached; we considered it your commitment to this project. And for that we say "thank you." We unfortunately had to limit the number of stories used. The time and effort many of you put into your submissions were fantastic. Although I didn't get the opportunity to speak to all of you personally, it was a great chance for me to see what you enjoy most about Northern California.

We did as much checking as humanly possible to make sure the places described in the book exist and are legitimate. But we apologize if errors slipped through. If there is a place of interest that catches your attention and the location is not defined in this book, please feel free to call your local Chamber of Commerce and/or Visitors Bureau; they can guide you to your destination. You may also call Office of Tourism in Sacramento at 1-800-862-2543. They have available a packet of informartion on the entire State which will include some of the areas you may be inquiring about.

To all travelers: Enjoy the book and always stay **"On The Go With KGO."**

BIG BROTHERS
BIG SISTERS

Big Brothers/Big Sisters is a nonprofit organization that is dedicated to serving children from single-parent family homes. This program is as elementary as putting a friend (a carefully screened adult volunteer) in a child's life, giving hope to a child's future.

In Northern California, the agencies match the Little Brothers and Little Sisters with Big Brothers and Big Sisters who have similar interests and who can act as positive support systems to them. The volunteers see the youths several times each month and act as friends and mentors while playing ball, going to the library, gardening, or pursuing whatever interests they both share. These dynamic relationships give Little Brothers and Little Sisters a greater sense of self-esteem and a more positive outlook on life.

For almost 100 years, Big Brothers/Big Sisters has been dedicated to assisting youth achieve their highest potential as they grow to become responsible men and women. The one-on-one relationship is focused on transforming lives and enriching families, communities and society.

Occasionally, our Big Brothers and Sisters, along with little Brothers and Sisters are treated royally. On Sunday, October 30, 1994, Big Brother Cassius Conliffe and Big Sister June Miller (both volunteer award winners for outstanding service) were selected to participate in a "Dream Date" along with their friends, Walter, 14, and Karin, 13. Capitol Records, in conjunction with BeBe and CeCe

700 Edgewater Dr., Suite 333 • Oakland, CA 94621

Continued, Page Two

Winnians, the outstanding gospel duo, picked up the tab for a day long extravaganza. The day included a splendid meal at Kincaid's Restaurant in historical Jack London Square. After dining on everything from grilled salmon to cheeseburgers, the foursome, accompanied by Public Relations Coordinator Rhonda White-Warner and her daughter Jahnee', 16, whisked off to Oakland's Paramount Theatre to hear the Grammy award winning brother and sister in concert.

The highlight of the evening was the privilege of being ushered backstage to meet the performers, collect autographs and take memorable photographs. Oakland was one of several cities selected to assist in the promotion of the duo's poignant single, "We Can make A Difference," which strongly encourages each of us to do what we can to assist others. Needless to say, for two young people, this memorable day will be one which will not be forgotten.

You can get involved by calling 1-800-288-4KID. We will tell you how you can become one of those committed volunteers who have made a difference in a child's life.

Photo: George Livingston, Jr.

Photo (l to r): BB Cassius Conliffe, CeCe and BeBe Winnians, BS June Miller, LS Karin. Seated in front LB Walter.

KGO Radio

Personalities

The KGO Radio Morning News Team

Jim Dunbar

You'll find Jim on the road...

If I tell you my favorite place to visit or thing to do in Northern California, then it won't be the best anymore, because everybody will go...so, I'm not going to tell!

However, the drive along Highway 1, either north or south, all the way to the big smoke stacks at Moss Landing in the south or up to Mendocino in the north, is unsurpassed. There are spots along the way that remind me of the Maine coast, which is spectacular. We're lucky to have this opportunity within a couple hours' drive.

Just don't try it on Saturday or Sunday, because that's when I'm out there!

Ted Wygant

Ted loves Sonoma ... everything about it.

My favorite place, as a lot of listeners know, is the town of Sonoma. I love the Plaza, for just sitting, or for a picnic. And, surrounding the Plaza you'll find whatever you want to eat at one of the several very fine restaurants.

From the Plaza you can walk to nearby Sebastiani Vineyards, where you can picnic among the vineyards. Or you can just enjoy the historic buildings, including the mission, the old barracks, and all of the other buildings in downtown Sonoma.

It's just a great place to spend a day or more -- or even to live there. I'd be happy forever being around Sonoma.

You won't find Joe following sports at his favorite retreat.

The Heritage House on Highway 1, just a few miles south of the town of Mendocino, is incredibly picturesque and overlooks the ocean. The area has a small, lovely cove. Every room is an individual cottage furnished with perfect taste, and almost all the cottages have fireplaces and in-room spas.

There are no telephones or televisions because they would only intrude on the fairy-tale beauty of the surroundings. There is no need to leave the resort for meals because the restaurant is superb. It is set in the classic manner. At breakfast you even get your own toaster!

By the way, for movie fans there are two cottages of some significance. They are right at the top of the cove, which is a beautiful spot. One cottage is named "Same Time," the other "Next Year." And, yes, that is where the movie "Same Time Next Year" was filmed about 20 years ago.

The cottage used in the movie "Same Time Next Year."

Joe Starkey

KGO Radio Sports Director

Rosie Allen

KGO Radio
Afternoon News Anchor

When she is not reporting the news, Rosie can be found at flea markets or at the newest of arts and crafts events.

I like to spend my weekends trooping through flea markets. I think it's a lot of fun, it gets me out of the house and is usually inexpensive; but then again it can also be very costly, depending on where you go. I especially like the one at Laney College in Oakland, because it's easy to get to, and it's close to home.

Other times, I'll go traipsing down to San Jose, up to Marin County, or out to other Bay Area locations. I'm a flea market junkie!

I also enjoy going to fairs and festivals, depending on the season. I just love checking out new arts and crafts. The things that people make are definitely interesting to me.

Original photo & effect by: Diana Petersen

An arts and crafts festival at Jack London Square in Oakland.

When it comes to favorite things to do, it all depends on if you're asking: with or without the kids?

When it comes to things to do, there are two separate categories: Whether my wife, Janet, and I are going alone, or whether the four kids are joining us.

Janet and I love to just get away for a night or two. We enjoy the Napa Valley just to see the countryside. We're not big wine drinkers, but Napa is so beautiful. We stay at several different places.

We also love going to Clear Lake. We've gone on a tennis package, where I play and she complains. We'll sometimes go with another couple.

With the kids, it's pretty much event or activity-centered. They like the Boardwalk at Santa Cruz, Great America and going to

The Baxters on their annual Christmas tree outing.

Alcatraz. We also spend time exploring around in San Francisco. We like Chinatown.

The one thing I pretty much demand as a family event occurs during the holidays, when we go out and cut down a Christmas tree. We usually go to Clayton Valley Tree Farm. We've done that for as long as I can remember, and we take pictures every year and watch the family grow. I don't know how long that's going to go on now, because everybody's moving out and going to college; but that's something we've had a lot of fun doing -- going out and disagreeing on which Christmas tree we're going to bring home.

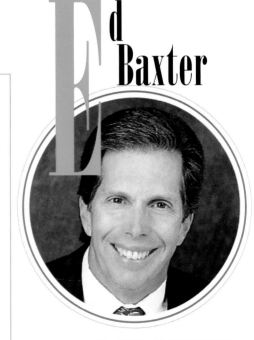

Ed Baxter

KGO Radio
Afternoon News Anchor

Ronn Owens

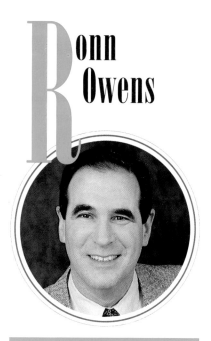

KGO Radio
Talk Show Host

A relaxing getaway... a little lunch, a little wine and a whole lot of Napa.

I would say that my favorite getaway spot is the Napa Valley because it tends to be much quieter than San Francisco. The time and the pace are a lot slower there.

I like to have a nice lunch out on the patio at Bistro Don Giovanni and sip some good wine.

I also love to go to Auberge du Soleil. It is such a great place to eat. (It's great, just as long as you take a second out on your mortgage!) But, seriously, it's a wonderful place, and is without a question the No. 1 spot.

Another recommendation is Opus One Winery. It's a winery partnership between the Mondavis and Rothchilds. If you ever get a chance to visit a winery, <u>that</u> is the one to see. It is absolutely magnificent, like a hi-tech castle.

Mike Shumann

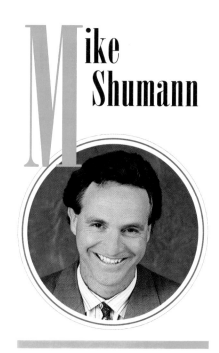

KGO Radio
Sports Reporter

When he's not talking sports, you'll find Mike at <u>The Inn.</u>

My favorite place in Northern California is the Little River Inn just south of the coastal town of Mendocino.

I was going up there one time to stay at another place, and it turned out we didn't like the place we were supposed to stay. So we just kept driving up the coast and found the Little River Inn.

It's absolutely beautiful -- right on the water. It's got little bungalows with fireplaces and whirlpools, a nine-hole golf course in the hills behind it, tennis courts and a fantastic restaurant. You don't have to leave the complex; it has it all. And the great news is you're only five minutes away from Mendocino, which of course is one of the most beautiful places in the world.

So if you ever get a chance for a getaway, I highly recommend The Little River Inn.

Brian Copeland

KGO Radio Talk Show Host

You'll find Brian at <u>his</u> favorite place doing his favorite thing when you go to...

One of my favorite places to go is in Livermore. I love camping and fishing, and I can't think of a better place to go than Lake Del Valle. I take my whole family. The kids love to splash around.

You can rent tents for camping, and there's even parking for trailers. You can usually get in without a reservation. However, if you feel more comfortable making reservations, you can make one on very short notice. It's inexpensive and close to town, just in case you need to run out and get some food or beer!

The lake is stocked so the fishing is great. It has bass, trout and catfish. Usually, my family and I spend a couple of weeks there every summer.

Chris Clarke

KGO Radio
Talk Show Host

For Chris, his back yard leads to hiking, running, surfing, bicycling...so why go anywhere else when your back yard is Stinson Beach.

Stinson Beach is probably the best place in Northern California for me because it has the ocean, the beach and the mountains. You can hang-glide, bicycle, surf and run. It offers the things that I get excited about.

I don't need to go hiking anywhere else because I can go hiking there. I don't need to run anywhere else because I go running there. I don't need to go bicycling anywhere else because I go bicycling there. I don't need to go swimming or surfing anywhere else because I've got it all there. Right in my back yard.

Plus, there are great places to eat in the area. The Station House Cafe in Point Reyes Station is a good place to

The waves go crashing to the shore at Stinson Beach.

go. And Tony's Restaurant, further up the coast, has good barbecue oysters.

Stinson Beach is where I spend most of my time.

There are so many great things to do in Northern California that it's difficult to choose just one.

There are so many great things to do in Northern California, but our favorite place is the Wine Country in Napa and Sonoma Counties. We love the square in the town of Sonoma. Typically, we'll pick up a little picnic food and go riding off. We stay at bed-and-breakfast inns and really enjoy traveling through the vineyards in the spring when the mustard is blooming, and in the autumn when the leaves are turning orange.

Good food, good wine, nice people, historic spots to see and places to just kick back and relax.

I guess it's easy to choose the place I enjoy the most. I would go there every week if I could!

Photo by: Diana Petersen

A dramatic night-shot of the Christian Brothers Winery.

Lynn Jimenez

KGO Radio
Business Reporter

Greg Edmonds

KGO Radio
East Bay Bureau Chief

When Greg's not reporting, he is reading, hiking and exploring with the kids.

I love to go anywhere that's different. From the deserts to the woods. And I like to watch people.

A good example is the time I went to Yosemite to cover a fire and a shooting. While reporting the stories, I ended up hanging out with a couple of park rangers. I enjoy watching people work, and seeing what they get involved in. I don't know if people normally do that, but I love doing it.

I love hiking, particularly on Mount Tamalpais and in areas of Mendocino County, and also in Mount Diablo State Park.

I've got kids, and one thing that I like to do with them is drive to a new location and simply explore. I don't particularly like tourist areas, but I do like to go to remote areas around the Bay Area.

The beauty and spendor of Mt. Tamalpais.

Take a tip from Jim and visit Sea Ranch or the Russian River area.

It's been several years since I've goofed off in Northern California, but I used to have some real favorite places.

Sea Ranch is spectacular. I rented a cabin at the main lodge. No television, no radio, no phone. I just sat by the fire and listened to the surf.

And going toward Nevada there is a great winter spot called Long Barn.

In the Russian River area of Sonoma County, I particularly enjoyed Guerneville. There is fantastic scenery in Little River, and there are absolutely unbelievable restaurants in Occidental.

If you want some real variety, there is the Featherbed Railroad Company in the town of Nice on Clear Lake in Lake County. Sleep in a railway caboose right on the lake. Call for reservations.

As I said, I visited all these places years ago. None of my information may apply today; times do change. But if these spots still exist, they are all musts.

The glorious sight of downtown Guerneville.

Photo by: Verne Paule

Jim Eason

KGO Radio Talk Show Host

Bill Wattenburg

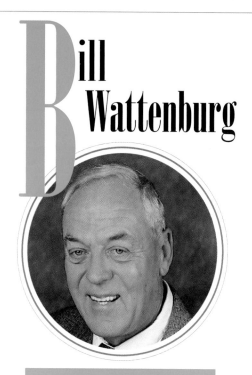

KGO Radio
Talk Show Host

The cleanest, nicest lake in the state is where you'll find Bill.

The cleanest, nicest lake in the whole state is Lake Almanor, which is not far from where I live. It has developed beautifully.

There's a place on the west side called the Pines, where there's a resort area and a restaurant called Fox's Lakeside Restaurant. It's sort of becoming world famous, and has attracted fantastic chefs who have relocated up in the mountains.

I like a lot of places in Northern California; but if I have a chance to go anywhere around the greater Lake Tahoe area, I go to Lake Almanor.

Pat Davis

KGO Radio
Sacramento Bureau Chief

When Pat is not in Sacramento, he is in Mendocino enjoying the beauty and cooler air.

My favorite place in Northern California is Mendocino. In just three and a half hours drive from Sacramento, it feels like you're in a different world.

I love to walk around the little town of Mendocino and I enjoy going to the Mendocino Headlands, where the spray of the surf shoots up as high as 150 feet. It is so breathtaking that it's beyond my ability to describe.

There are many fine restaurants. And you're not that far from Fort Bragg, which has some very nice restaurants as well.

The best place to stay in Mendocino is Little River Lodge. It's pricey, but each room has a view of the ocean and its own fireplace. Since it can be 105 degrees at home in Sacramento, the greatest feeling of all after a day of sightseeing along the coast is to go back to the lodge and start a fire in the fireplace -- in the middle of August!

Another favorite getaway is in the Gold Country of the Sierra foothills. The best places to stay in the Gold Country are charming bed and breakfast inns. They're all over the place.

I particularly like the towns of Grass Valley, Nevada City, Sonora, Jackson and Amador City which are filled with things to do. There are antique shops and great restaurants. The towns have maintained that old-town feel and there's a real sense of community, too. Each town has its own personality and identity.

The towns have nice little inns, shops, restaurants and pizza parlors.

Photos by: Verne Paule

Above: Dogs romping in the cool, refreshing waters of Mendocino.
Below: The picturesque Blow Hole in the Mendocino Headlands.

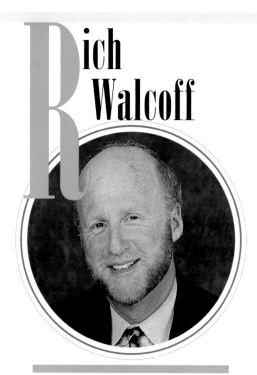

Rich Walcoff

KGO Radio
Associate Sports Director

You'll find Rich at <u>his</u> favorite place: Point Reyes Seashore

The dream day in Northern California for me is to take some good friends or family and head out to Point Reyes National Seashore and Tomales Bay in Marin County.

On certain days, you can have the beach all to yourself. I like Lemon Tour Beach. I like to take a good hike and walk along the water and watch the waves and look for whales and just take in the view. And then, later in the afternoon, enjoy barbecued oysters and drink microbrews.

I also really enjoy Indian Head Beach, which you have to hike over hills to reach. It's got some teepees along the water which my boys really enjoy. They run around and simulate the Wild West.

Out on Tomales Bay, you can also take a paddle boat or raft. It's more calm than the Pacific Ocean.

Scenic Drakes Beach at Point Reyes National Seashore.

Photo by: Verne Paule

In This Section...

HIGH SIERRA

NORTH COAST

THE BAY AREA

GOLD COUNTRY

CENTRAL COAST

SHASTA CASCADE

MENDOCINO

Picturesque, scenic, quaint, historic, fascinating, and not too far from the Bay Area -- it's Mendocino, about 150 miles north of San Francisco and overlooking the Pacific Ocean. It is located on Highway 1 and eas-ily accessible by driving north on Highway 101 to Cloverdale, and then west on Highway 128 to Highway 1, past a number of lovely ranches, wineries, towns, several miles of stately redwoods in the Mendocino forest and the meandering Navarro River that empties into the ocean.

A coastal view of historic Mendocino.

Photo by: Verne Paule

Mendocino has a New England atmosphere with many Victorian houses and businesses. There are many excellent restaurants, bed-and-breakfast inns in the vicinity, as well as the old, well-preserved Mendocino Hotel on Main Street, which has a four-star restaurant and many antiques.

There are many interesting shops, boutiques, art galleries and two museums. One is the Ford House, built in 1854 and named for Jerome B. Ford, the acknowledged founder of Mendocino. It can be seen as the sheriff's station on TV's "Murder, She Wrote," and serves as also the town's Visitors Center.

Across Main Street is the Kelley House Museum, built in 1861 by William H. Kelley. Both museums highlight the lumber industry that still flourishes in and around Mendocino.

There is a seashore park and beach at the end of Main Street that is very photogenic with its eroded arch and magnificent view of Mendocino from the trails leading down to the beach. Fog sometimes makes the town of Mendocino quite mystic; but, in contrast, the sunshine and a sky filled with colorful cumulous clouds make it a picturesque paradise of Northern California.

Submitted by Verne Paule

Six miles west of Willits an obscure dirt road leaves Highway 20 and meanders its way through a beautiful forested valley. This scenic road eventually ends at a 400-acre oasis bordering the Noyo River. The sanctuary is called Redwood Forest Ranch.

Here, far away from people and cars, the deer and other wildlife abound. You'll find pristine moun tain air to breath, clean spring water, soothing sounds and stars bright enough to touch. This is a place to explore and experience nature. There are miles of hiking trails, beautiful river scenery and great mountain biking.

The accommodations consist of two "rustic" cabins (no TV and you may have to chop a little firewood), which combined can accommodate between 8-12 people. But almost more impressive than the scenery are the owners, Charles and Vanna Rae Bello. A retired architect and teacher, they have been working on this refuge for 27 years, and their tireless and passionate work is evident throughout the property. They are living a successful "back-to-nature" life and serve as an inspiration to all who visit. They are true California pioneers.

Submitted by
Charles & Vanna Rae Bello

One of our favorite places to go for a weekend of relaxation is a beautiful inn called the Heritage House in Little River. This romantic inn is located right outside the town of Mendocino.

nursery, which is stocked with beautiful plants and is open to all. Also located on the property are an art showroom, gift shop and a dress shop. There are no televisions or phones and, believe me,

to a private patio. The flower-adorned patio overlooks an ocean inlet covered by a huge eucalyptus tree. The room has a wood-burning fireplace, and in the bathroom is a double jacuzzi tub set next to a bay

More Great Places To Go From KGO...

The property itself is made up of acres and acres of beautiful coastside covered with flowers and trees. The rooms are arranged in small clusters throughout the acreage. Each room is given its own name and is unique in setting and decor. They range from simple to elegant depending on one's tastes and budget. Walking along the many paths found on the property you discover a lovely duck pond at one site, a gazebo overlooking the cliffside at another, a wooden stairway down to a rocky beach, and meadows of flowers. Many of these flowers are grown on site at the

you don't miss them.

Our favorite room is named the Cliffhouse 2. It is a lightly decorated room in mauve and off-white colors. The furniture is antique. It has a wall of glass with sliding doors opening

window overlooking the inlet. It's fantastic.

Included in the price of your stay is dinner and breakfast at the

Top: Relax, eat or just play games at the cozy Redwood Forest Ranch.

Left: The Cliffside Gazebo is a romantic hideaway at the charming Heritage House in Little River.

restaurant, which overlooks the ocean. There is both inside and outside dining. The menu changes daily and the food is absolutely delicious. Our favorite thing to do is to take our dessert back to our room, light a fire and sit listening to the crashing waves outside our room. What more can we say: the Heritage House has it all. It's a wonderful place to stay.

Submitted by Jeff & Sue Miller

We are frequent travelers and have had fun combining one of our favorite sites in Northern California with one of our favorite television shows.

For a Memorial Day weekend getaway, we had the pleasure of traveling north to Mendocino. What a lovely town this is. Not spoiled by over-commercialization, Mendocino retains its small-town image, with magnificent craggy cliffs overlooking a wild,

white-capped sea (at least it was this way during our stay). Locals told us of calm waters at times, too.

We wandered along the Mendocino headlands, enjoying the refreshing breezes and taking in the scenery. Further down the headlands, but still along the shore, we came upon a gardener's paradise of white calla lillies—all growing wild and wonderful.

After an invigorating walk, we were enchanted by the welcoming fireplace at the Hill House, the inn often featured in "Murder, She Wrote." We stayed overnight and were pleased with the rooms, all were furnished in period style (keeping with the overall appearance of the inn and indeed with Mendocino itself—gracious and charming). We look forward to our next visit to this quaint town on the North Coast.

Submitted by Annie Zadany & Elizabeth Cicchini

We live on the west coast of Florida, and we visit our daughter (Joyce Emory) in California at least once per year and usually stay for several weeks. During our visit we always make it a point to stay a few days at the Mendocino Hotel. We prefer to have room No. 1, one of the rooms with its window opening toward the bay and ocean. The window opens to the second-floor deck. The deck is a great place to have our evening happy hour.

The sunsets are beautiful and much different from ours in Florida. We don't normally have the fog, which here adds to the view. In addition, the town of Mendocino and its history add greatly to the feeling of contentment.

We usually arrive from the East Bay on Sunday afternoon, just

about when most people are leaving to go back to the city. My husband, Irish, and I park our car and don't get back into it until it's time to go home. We spend our days browsing through the shops and strolling along the cliffs above the surf. Even when it is foggy, this is one of the greatest places on earth. In fact, the fog increases the ambi-

The Mendocino Hotel

ance. The coolness is a welcome relief from the Florida heat.

Walking along the edge of the meandering cliff we go north from the town and, just before reaching Route 1, we turn right up a grass-covered road to the top of a hill. This road seems to be known to only a few tourists, but is a favorite for the locals. At the top of the hill is the high school. There cannot be a sports field in the world with such a view. On a clear day one can see for miles. Further to the north, you can see the lighthouse seen in the TV show "Murder, She Wrote."

Back in town we stop at the local grocery store and purchase our happy-hour treats. A little ice from the hotel kitchen and we're ready to take our seats for the greatest show on earth. The hotel provides comfortable chairs, we provide the drinks and treats, God provides the rest.

As the sun sets over the Pacific fog, we sip our wine and consider how lucky we are to have this opportunity. After more than fifty years of marriage, we feel fortunate to be able to enjoy so much together.

Submitted by Ruth & Irish Lay

When I want to unwind, I head for the Mendocino Coast and a house on a windswept bluff above the sea. Sirenisea (South Mendocino) and Mendocino Coast Rentals (Mendocino North) both have some lovely private homes for rent, by the weekend or the week.

Most have ocean views and come complete with kitchen utensils, linens, barbecues, stereos, and microwave ovens. Some have hot tubs and beach access. Some even boast private beaches, lovely coves, dazzling panoramas of sunset over spray-splashed craggy rocks, and lots of peace and privacy.

Costs vary from $85-$250 per night, and most rental companies offer three-for-two deals (three nights for the price of two), or special off-season rates.

Most homes sleep from 4-8 people, so you can bring the family or get together with friends. Some homes even accept pets.

Bring your own food and plan menus in advance so you don't

A fantastic view of the Mendocino coast.

forget vital ingredients (some homes are lean in the condiment department), and also bring your beach towels, a few good books, and relax.

If you get cabin fever, there's always a beach to stroll or Mendocino Village to explore. Try Sunday brunch at Cafe Beaujolais

or the Chocolate Moose.

One thing. Please don't go there on *my* weekend. I like my privacy, you know?

Submitted by Mary Lynn Archibald

Whether you're 5 or 95, you don't want to miss one of the real jewels of the North Coast: the wonderful but hidden Montgomery Woods State Park, a 1,484-acre stand of virgin redwoods.

Montgomery Woods may be reached from Highway 1 by taking the Comptche-Ukiah Road and going about 30 winding but beautiful miles; or off Highway 101 in Ukiah, take Orr Springs Road 15 miles west.

Entering the redwood grove is like walking into a natural cathedral, especially in the spring when wildflowers are abundant. It's a wonderful place to hike, to picnic, or just to gawk at the enormous trees that dominate the forest. It has well-marked hiking trails, many following Montgomery Creek. Or you can climb the old logging road and have a spectacular view of the canyon below. The woods are filled with sword, wood and broken ferns. Growing alongside the redwoods are Douglas fir, tan oak, madrone and chinquapin. The silence of the forest is often broken by a woodpecker or a steller's jay. You can't help but feel calm, refreshed and at peace as you walk along the trails. It is a feeling that remains with you long after you've left the park, too. Don't miss this.

Submitted by Sylvia Eiffert

Our favorite place to go to relax is Sea Ranch, located on Highway 1 approximately two-and-a-half hours north of San Francisco, just a little south of the town of Gualala.

It is nature's best, and the scenery getting there is just as beautiful. Sea Ranch boasts of deer, whales, sea lions, small wild animals and wildflowers that will take

Fishing is terriffic at Sea Ranch!

your breath away. It has homes with views and hot tubs.

All of nature and wildlife are preserved, and there are hiking trails, horse trails and a nine-hole golf course. The fishing is great, even in the rain. One can improvise for rain gear. It's peaceful and serene– the best place to unwind.

Submitted by Paige Gilpin

Northern California has so many things to do and places to see it is difficult to select a favorite, but visits to wineries and the vineyards in the wine country are always enjoyable. During the past three years the highlight of our trips has been to visit our adopted grapevine, which we named Philo P. Noir D'Vine, at Obester Winery in the beautiful Anderson Valley in Mendocino County.

Obester Winery has an "Adopt-a-Vine" program, and each June the proud parents of adopted vines gather for a full-scale birthday party to celebrate and visit with their vines, compare notes, brag about their growth, and introduce each other to new members of the family.

Our first party at the winery in 1992 was a picnic with about 100

vine parents. Many who could not come sent cards and gifts, which were on display and placed by their vines in the vineyard. This year's party was attended by nearly 400 parents and guests as the family continues to grow.

One of the obvious benefits of being a vine parent is that it gives us another reason to visit the wine country more often. Although it is only a couple hours drive from

The Obester Winery Tasting Room in Philo.

San Francisco, we usually try and stay at one of the local bed-and-breakfast inns so we can relax and enjoy the beautiful and peaceful surroundings.

Photo by: Kurt Bjorkquist

We also receive two bottles of wine each year, along with letters from our vine telling us how he is doing during the year, and of course, the invitation to the Birthday Party when all the adopted vines are dressed up with balloons and ribbons in the vineyard.

We enjoy all the beautiful areas of Northern California, and this gives us an added reason to visit them.

Submitted by
Dave & Carol Amaral

If you are dreaming of a weekend in Hawaii but can't quite make it, how about the next closest place? At Point Arena, the old lighthouse and museum are run by a non-profit group. They have three cottages, modest but enchanting, which are available for rent.

It's remote, yes, and beautiful, whether you are into watching whales, birds, or just the fog rolling in over the surf. Personally, I am quite happy watching the surf. Within easy driving distance there

are many good restaurants from Mendocino in the north to Gualala in the south, and stretching between is that ever-beautiful coastline.

For those interested in vineyards and the juice of the grape, try a most scenic drive through beautiful rural Anderson Valley, returning to the coast on Highway 128 with its magnificent groves of redwood trees along the Navarro River.

Submitted by Sheila P. Dundon

SONOMA

Healdsburg, located just 70 miles above San Francisco in the heart of the Sonoma Wine Country, is a beautiful destination for anyone. If you're a family with young children, a honeymooning couple, or on your own for a weekend getaway, there's something for everyone.

The Russian River, the main attraction of Healdsburg, has many

a lovely spot to boat, swim, picnic or fish. Whether you like the deep, beach-like swimming hole at Veterans Memorial Park, or the more rustic spots where the locals go up Fitch Mountain Road, you can find a spot just right for you.

But it's not just the river that draws people to Healdsburg. The beautiful little town has everything from lovely restaurants, bakeries and stores, to the many great wineries in the vicinity. And don't forget to check out the lovely Old Victorians up on West Grant Street, or the beautiful Spanish-style plaza in the center of town.

Submitted by Sally Smith

Photo by: Verne Paule

Top: Russian River offers many activities like swimming, fishing and boating at the Johnson Beach.

Bottom: Sheila Dundon has a "birds-eye" view of Point Arena's lighthouse.

I wanted to point out a great little adventure we do every summer in Sonoma County, near Healdsburg.

We hook up with an outfitter called Getaway Bike Tours, and it takes us on a great morning bike tour of small wineries in the Dry Creek Valley. The guides are the owners, and they really know their stuff. They always make us a delicious home-cooked gourmet picnic lunch under the redwoods. It's really nice. After lunch we get

This famous Bodega Bay shot is where the Hitchcock thriller "The Birds" was filmed.

Photo by: Verne Paule

shuttled in vans to a special launch spot on the Russian River, and we have a great time going down the river in canoes. We stop for swims and flow down with the rapids. Lots of fun on a hot day.

This year we'll go with the kids. I am sure they will love it.

Ask for the Pedal 'N' Paddle trip, and at $89 it is well worth it. Getaway Bike Tours' phone number is 800-499-2453.

Submitted by Carina Wonn

A favorite spot of mine is Bodega Bay.

Artist's hideaway, honeymoon retreat, or jump-off place for the Sonoma Wine Country, Bodega Bay is all this and more. I am an artist, and I come here for the laid-back atmosphere, the bay and ocean, and the chance to renew away from the everyday clamor.

At Bodega Bay you can beachcomb at Doran Beach and Salmon Creek, and dine at the restaurants on salmon and fish chowder. Or play golf, visit art galleries and antique shops, watch whales and the fishing fleet. Bodega Bay is very busy but fun during its annual fish-

ing festival. The rest of the year it is truly a hideaway spot.

It is 68 miles from San Francisco up Highway 101 to Petaluma, then out the Bodega Highway to Highway 1 and down through a coastal canyon to the bay. Make reservations for the luxurious Inn at the Tides or the Bodega Bay Lodge, even for the modest and comfortable Bodega Harbor Inn. If you find you love the area as much as I do, there are vacation rental homes available for a week at the ocean.

Submitted by Charlotte Teeples

My wife and I have just returned from a beautiful day at Morton's Warm Springs, a day resort about four miles north of Glen Ellen, on Warm Springs Road in Sonoma County. The resort has been around since about 1900.

Warm springs bubble up to feed the three swimming pools, hence the name. There is a kiddie pool for wading, a medium-sized pool for kids and adults, and a large pool with a diving board.

There are also many picnic tables under large trees, a game room with pinball machines, video games and air hockey.

On the grounds, there are a baseball field, a basketball court and a large lawn area for sunbathing.

I've been going there since I was a child, and now go there with my wife and occasionally with my nieces. Admission is $3.50 for

Family fun at Morton's Warm Springs.

Photo by: Verne Paule

adults on weekdays, $5 on weekends and holidays. Morton's is open from May to October.

Glen Ellen is beautiful, too. A wonderful place to stay is the Gaige House Inn on Arnold Drive about a quarter-mile north of Warm Springs Road. Lovely, large rooms, beautifully furnished. The largest room also has a large bathroom with a large bathtub. It's reasonably priced for a wine country inn.

Submitted by Paul Zawilski

Sometimes, you need to be impulsive. This daytime getaway is for just such an occasion. If you wake up on a weekend and the weather is gorgeous, forget about cleaning the house and head over to Glen Ellen in Sonoma County. There you will find the Jack London State Historic Park. The park was created in 1959 and now includes more than 800 acres, with picnic areas and hiking trails.

When you first arrive, visit the House of Happy Walls. This is the museum that houses Jack London's possessions and tells about the life of the world-famous author. Then take the half-mile walk through the oaks and redwoods to the remains of Wolf House. This is the amazing house that London and his wife, Charmain, planned and had built in 1913. Right before they

Remains of the Wolf House at Jack London State Park.

The gravesite of Jack London.

were going to move in, the house mysteriously burned to the ground. No one knows what caused the dev-

astating fire, but it is believed to have been deliberately set. The ruins themselves are impressive, and not to be missed. A short distance away is the grave site. Jack London's ashes were buried on a hill near the graves of two pioneer children. A red boulder from the ruins of Wolf House was placed on top.

Submitted by Janet G. Lampe

Our favorite place to go in Northern California is Little Switzerland in El Verano in Sonoma County. The owners of this dancing and dining place are Yves and Annette Casabonne.

Not a fancy place, but a quaint place that brings us happiness, friends, wonderful music for dancing and listening. Each week there are different bands to play polka, waltz, Latin and swing music.

Hanna's Kitchen serves light snacks and meals. Annie, 96 years

young, has been dancing at Little Switzerland for 54 years. Carl Genter is 94 and taking polka danc-

Annette and Don enjoying their time together at Little Switzerland.

ing lessons. They are weekly dancers at Little Switzerland. It is a place to have fun and meet new people. People from all over the world visit Little Switzerland.

On occasion, Ted Wygant, KGO morning news, talks about polka music, accordions and Little Switzerland.

Please join us one weekend and enjoy our "Favorite Place On The Go" at Little Switzerland in El Verano.

Submitted by Annette & Don Perry

WINE COUNTRY

You look at your watch and wait, your eyes scanning a large fissure on top of a pile of black lava rock. Suddenly, it blows. Water and steam, 350 degrees hot, shoot about 60 feet into the air. It recedes, then jets high in the air again, up and down for about four minutes. Repeat performances of this natural phenomenon will average about 40 minutes apart, 24 hours a day, year after year.

California's Old Faithful ranks among the world's few geysers that go off at regular intervals. It performs faithfully because of ideal geological conditions that exist deep underground. Essentially, a natural source of water flows over hot magma, boils and collects in large cavities. Tremendous pressures then build and force steam and water through fissures to the surface. Since these conditions remain fairly constant, Old Faithful erupts regularly.

It is located in the foothills of Mount St. Helena, in the beautiful upper Napa Valley wine country, 78 miles north of San Francisco. Open 365 days, it has a snack bar, gift shop, picnic area and tour rates.

Submitted by Dawn Agapoff

We enjoy horseback riding as a family activity when we go on vacation, and we were so pleased to find a wonderful stable so close to us that offered some of the most beautiful trails in the country. Not only was the ride outstanding, but the guides were so friendly and helpful, and the horses were very well cared for and seemed to enjoy the ride as much as we did.

We contacted Sonoma Cattle Co. and made reservations to go to Jack London State Park in Glen Ellen. It is located about one hour north of the Golden Gate Bridge in the Sonoma Wine Country. The riding trails ascend from deep redwood forests with springs and every kind of fern native to the area, to ridge tops views that reach for miles.

The day was enhanced by the friendly service we received (a commodity not always offered in this day and age), and their genuine concern for our well-being. I have recommended this company to several of my friends, and they also endorse this stable.

Submitted by Kelly D. Eder

In a recent December, a friend and I, having finished our Christmas preparations, decided the Sunday before Christmas to drive to Napa and ride on the Napa Valley Wine Train. This was a great time to go because there were fewer people, and there was the added bonus of seeing the Christmas lights, especially in Yountville.

The round trip is three hours. We had a gift certificate for the deli car, which is $20 per person. The food was delicious, and there was great service. In addition to the dining cars, there are the wine-tasting and lounge cars. All of the cars have been beautifully restored with polished mahogany, brass and etched glass.

There are wonderful views of the wineries and the Napa Valley. The next day we visited some of the wineries and bought a few bottles of wine. We also drove to Yountville to visit the great bottle shops at Washington Square, and we ate in a great deli. That night we saw the Christmas lights, which were beautiful.

While in Napa we stayed at the Chateau Hotel. It has a nice breakfast buffet, and in the evening there is wine-tasting.

We had a wonderful time. It is a great way to relax and get away from all the Christmas rush.

Submitted by Dorothy J. Levin

The Bay Area is filled with fantastic places to visit. There are also too many choices to pick one that is uniquely special. However, my favorite getaway is the Silverado Country Club and

Above: Having fun at Beringer Winery.
Right: Playing golf at Silverado C.C. in Napa.

Beringer Winery in Napa Valley. Just an hour or so out of the city and you're in the most beautiful, scenic countryside. The sky is so clear and blue it almost doesn't look real. The white, puffy clouds roll by and you want to touch them.

Silverado has so much charm and old-fashioned gentility. It really lends itself as a very relaxed and peaceful place to spend a weekend, as well as play a great round of golf.

Napa Valley is a lovely back-drop for any activity you want to engage in. From mud baths to glider-flying, wine-tasting to ballooning, golf to train rides, it has it all.

Beringer is a particularly attractive winery with a good wine tour. However, the Napa Valley has so many wineries to choose from — like Sterling or Domaine Chandon. There are also great places to eat, like Auberge du Soleil or Tra Vigne and nice resorts in the area, like the Sonoma Mission Inn and Spa or the Meadowood Resort.

Submitted by Gail Kusudo

DEL NORTE

Leaving the summer heat of Arizona, I find the beautiful, cool coastal area of Northern California a most welcome relief. The added bonus is the magnificence of the redwoods, which I understand are found only in California.

The Trees of Mystery, located 15 miles south of Crescent City, with its trail of unusual trees, the redwood carvings telling the stories of Paul Bunyan and his men, as well as the history of the redwoods, make this a most interesting and beautiful place to visit.

Then to find an Indian Museum of such magnitude makes me want to spend hours absorbing the arts, crafts and cultures of Native Americans. A plaque from the California Historical Society was given to this museum for preserving California history.

A three-star motel and fine restaurant make it easy for me to stay over and enjoy a beautiful two-mile hike through the Redwood National Park to an ocean beach.

For all these reasons, I am drawn to the redwood country, and especially to the Trees of Mystery, truly the jewel of the Redwood Highway.

Submitted by Jack Grisinger

California's Old Faithful erupts every 40 minutes.

Take a ride on the Napa Valley Wine Train.

NORTH COAST

Located six hours from either the Bay Area or Sacramento, the Redwood National Park has been our yearly destination for the past 15 years. It's nestled on the new Highway 101 bypass called the Newton B. Drury Parkway. This is one place that shouldn't be missed, and will not be forgotten.

Driving north to the park, you will soon see the famous Prairie lined with parking strips to view the magnificent elk herds. This is a great photographic opportunity, with the elk lazily eating among a field of grass and wildflowers.

Just to the right of the park entrance is the visitor's center and the trailhead for many miles of hiking trails. There are two mountain-bike trails available, as well as the Relevation Trail for the blind and disabled. A must hike is the James Irvine trail to one of the hidden wonders of California -- Fern Canyon. This fairly easy 11-mile hike takes you through old-growth redwoods, past dedicated groves, over streams, and eventually to Gold Bluff Beach. As you near the ocean, the trail drops down into the small canyon covered with millions of

James Irvine Trail, at Prairie Creek State Park in Orick.

ferns, petite waterfalls, and a lovely little creek running through it.

If walking is not your style, take Davidson Road just south of the park, and drive to Gold Bluff Beach. This is a winding gravel road, so make sure you take your time. A herd of elk spend all year at the beach, and the road crosses two small creeks to the Fern Canyon parking lot. It's a leisurely one-mile stroll through the canyon.

Nearby activities are the River, Crescent City, Orick Beach, and Patrick's State Park. Couples and families are sure to enjoy this special spot. ***Submitted by Cathy M. Long***

HUMBOLDT

Located on the coast of southern Humboldt County is Shelter Cove, which lies between Fort Bragg and Eureka.

The Beachcomber Inn is a great base to explore the King Range National Conservation Area, with its beautiful black-sand beach to the summit of King Peak which at 4,086 feet is the highest mountain in the Coast Range. Bordering the Conservation Area to the south, discover the Sinkyone Wilderness Area, with its wild beauty, herd of Roosevelt elk, miles of trails, and 100-year-old ranch house.

Black Sand Beach at Shelter Cove.

Shelter Cove offers whale-watching, tide pools, safe swimming beach (no undertow), surfing and fishing (salmon and bottom fish). Spring months offer great perch (red tail) fishing from the beach.

The Beachcomber Inn is located a short walk from the south tiedown area of the 2,800-foot air strip and Cove Beach. All units have barbecues, picnic tables and more.

Submitted by Thomas & Marilyn Machi

One of the most beautiful spots in Northern California is located near the town of Garberville on the Avenue of the Giants and along the Eel River.

The Benbow Inn is a beautiful hotel, a National Historical Landmark, magnificently furnished and decorated with antiques. It has very comfortable beds and modern bathrooms. It reminded us of a very elegant European hotel.

The dining room, food and service all were tops. There is a terrace for eating outside, and a beautiful lawn with deck chairs to relax. There are no televisions in the rooms, but there is a decanter of wine and a basket full of reading material instead. And classic films are shown nightly.

Submitted by Joyce & Bill Remak

There is a plant with very showy flowers, that with the exception of a few places in Oregon and perhaps Baja California, is only found in California.

This is the Western Azalea, or Occidental, which in Northern California is at its peak on Memorial Day weekend. The flower color is pink and white, often in a

The beautiful Benbow Inn.

candystripe pattern, and the upper petal is orange, yellow and sometimes pink.

The best place to see the Western Azalea is Stagecoach Hill, a part of Dry Lagoon State Park,

located on Kane Road off Highway 101 between Patrick's Point State Park and the town of Orick. There is approximately a quarter-mile loop trail that takes you through the Azaleas.

Submitted by Mike McCullough

I love the North Coast in the fall, and my favorite part of the North Coast is the Trinidad area.

The combination of sandy beaches and towering redwoods makes visiting this area a unique and enchanting experience.

Patrick's Point State Park, with its agate beach, huge spiritual rocks and fog-shrouded coast, is a full day's adventure. Big and Little Lagoons are wonderful places to bird-watch or just enjoy a solitary walk on the sandy beach.

The endless expanse of Gold Beach with its pounding surf and the beauty of Fern Canyon make up for the bumpy ride necessary to get there. And the redwoods! Park after park of these wonderful trees, each

with its own unique features.

Eureka and Ferndale are close by for shopping and Victorian viewing.

For dining out, you can choose from a variety of restaurants, ranging from the casual Sea Scape at the wharf to the gourmet Larrupin' on Patrick's Point Road.

Accommodations run from camping to luxury bed-and-breakfast inns;

The beautiful Western Azalea is at its best during the Memorial Day Weekend.

but my favorite places to stay are the Bishop Pine Lodge, with its charming cabins, and the wonderful Lost Whale Bed-and-Breakfast, which serves the most delicious and varied breakfasts that I have ever had.

Submitted by Bonnie Meyer

MOTHER LODE

The Hotel Leger was one of those unique finds that one just happens to stumble upon while touring the Gold Rush country. In an attempt to get away from the throngs of tourists that converged upon the more larger towns like Jackson and Sonora, we happened upon the historic town of Mokelumne Hill. There we found the Hotel Leger. A true historic Gold Rush era hotel that retained much of the times in its decor.

Our room was beautifully appointed, and with the fireplace,

Welcome to the newly renovated Hotel Leger.

most romantic. The new owners (Mark and Nancy Jennings) will give a tour of the hotel. We found each room to have its own unique character in its decor. This area of California has now become quite famous for its wine production. After all these accolades, I have saved the best for last. The Hotel Leger has an early California Cuisine Restaurant. The restaurant at the Hotel Leger serves one of the finest oak-pit barbecue entrees featuring steak, fish, pork chops, chicken, and for those who prefer only vegetables, an all vegetarian menu. The price was quite reasonable, as were the room rates.

Since that initial visit we have returned to Mokelumne Hill and the Hotel Leger a number of times and have never been disappointed in our stay. On one of our visits a local theatrical company was putting on a play in the Hotel's Theater. So it is without hesitation that I heartily recommend the Hotel Leger to your readers.

Oh, and, by the way, the Hotel is *haunted*–which, of course, greatly adds to the atmosphere.

Submitted by Simone Musa

DOWNIENVILLE

My preference of a place to get away is Downienville in the Sierra's Mother Lode country. It was the first capitol of California and is full of history.

The town is located between the Yuba and American rivers, and has two very old bridges on each side, making it all very picturesque. It also sits between two mountains.

The accommodations are very reasonable. Children are welcome at the Riverside Motel. The other motel is a charming residence. Both are right in town, facing the Yuba River. Both are a stone's throw from the river so you can be lulled to sleep.

There are two dinner houses and a coffee shop for breakfast. There's also a pizza shop. You should try the bakery in town, famous for its danish and tarts. Be sure and try the Squaw bread; there's nothing else like it.

At the dinner houses, one can sit out on decks overlooking the river and listen to the gentle roar. Prices are reasonable. Reservations should be made, especially in the summer months.

At Christmas time the whole town celebrates for a week. The ladies wear bonnets, and the men dress in the fashion of the Gold Rush days.

The town is very clean and orderly with beautiful surroundings. The people are very friendly and are proud of their town. They won't hesitate to tell you so. I've just returned from my fourth visit (in 10 years). Something draws me back.

You should visit the General Store; their slogan is: "If we don't have it, you don't need it."

There are many lakes in the area that are excellent for fishing. Have a great time when visiting this paradise.

Submitted by Alice Brooks

NEVADA CITY

One place everyone can hike whether they are young, old or even in a wheelchair is six miles west of Nevada City on Highway 49 along the Independence Trail.

The trail follows the flumes that were built in the 1800s to carry water 25 miles to Smartville for hydraulic mining. The trail, built by volunteers, is accessible to wheelchairs for the first half-mile.

You actually walk on some of the rebuilt flumes overlooking the East Fork of the Yuba River. Springtime is the best time because the wildflowers are in bloom.

Submitted by Glorie Russell

Our favorite place, and not just because our son and his family live there, is the area around Grass Valley and Nevada City. Although we've seen tremendous growth over the years, that small town feeling where people greet each other on the street still prevails. It's nestled in the wooded foothills and offers both summer and winter outdoor recreation.

Nevada City also offers many interesting shops, fine theatre presentations and charming bed-and-breakfast inns. The Northern Queen Inn in Nevada City is our favorite place to stay. We especially enjoy the secluded chalets near the babbling brook. It's a friendly place with an absolutely superb restaurant.

Submitted by Mr. & Mrs. Lawrence Sommers

GRASS VALLEY

If I could choose a special place for a day or two in North-

ern California, I would take my easel, paints and a small suitcase and head for the area around Grass Valley, filled with delightful vistas and small journeys back in time.

Grass Valley has all the amenities

Left: Firehouse No.2 in Nevada City.

Below: Mountain lilac, Scotch bloom along Independence Trail in Nevada City.

of modern living. Shopping is great. There are numerous small shops with art and craft items, antiques and boutique articles. There are museums and a good many eateries (most of them feature a meat pie from old mining days called a "pasty"). Live theatre and concerts are presented in the Old Nevada Theatre. A favorite painting spot of mine is Fire House Number 1.

Other intriguing places to visit in the surrounding area include one of the nation's oldest covered bridges and hiking trails, full of fall foliage or spring wildflowers. There are also a variety of places of historical interest, where enthusiastic volunteers are available to answer questions and make your visit even more interesting and fun.

Submitted by Bernice Bywater

Rendering by: Bywater

Firehouse No. 1

EMPIRE MINE

I can't talk enough about the Gold Country! It's an all-year recreation area. Initially, one should be adventurous and explore the entire area by traveling along Highway 49, stopping at any of the appealing small towns with their many antique stores, boutiques, gift shops, museums, and other interesting places.

Once you've familiarized yourself with the area and its history, then you can really enjoy the many special events held year round. Among my favorites are the Frog Jumping Contest in Angels Camps, Daffodil Hill near Volcano, and the Indian Pow-Wow at Indian Grinding Rock State Park. I am especially fond of Nevada City. It's a quaint gold rush town in a beautiful setting.

The nearby Empire Mine is fascinating. A nice picnic area is provided. It's always fun to plan a picnic either before or after touring the area.

Submitted by Marcia Smith

MOANING CAVERN

If the spirit of adventure calls, take a trip to Moaning Cavern near the town of Murphys in the Gold Country.

Touring the cavern on foot is an awesome experience, but if you want to get the adreneline going, take the rappel tour. Rappelling offers the timid adventurer a chance to be Sylvester Stallone, if only for a few hours.

Moaning Cavern, an Indian

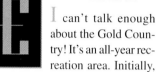

Home belonging to William Bourne Jr., owner of the Empire Mine.

burial site, is the largest public cavern chamber in California. Some of the oldest human remains in the United States have been found here.

After being outfitted with hard hat and gloves and listening to a brief equipment orientation, Phillip and I, novices to the sport, stepped into a harness with a rope comfortably secured to solid rock and ready to plunge 180 feet. Cavern walls encircled us during the first part of our descent as we carefully lowered ouselves down, feet

The Culvers just hanging around.

braced against hard rock. After passing through a narrow tunnel, we found ourselves dangling in an enormous cave filled with exquisite rock formations.

The maneuvering over the rest of the descent was a breeze. All we had to do was lower ourselves down to the cavern floor and marvel at the beauty and mystery around us.

***Submitted by
Karen & Phillip Culver***

A TRIP THRU GOLD COUNTRY

Gtrip through The Gold Country browsing the charming towns and staying in 150-year-old hotels makes a delightful jaunt back in time. Highlights from several excursions to the area include Jamestown, with its lovely Jamestown Hotel, and Columbia State Historic State Park. City Hotel accommodations include a room with antique furnishings, afternoon sherry, breakfast, a great old bar and gourmet dining. Main Street is fascinating with Gold Rush shops, a

Main street in Jamestown.

blacksmith shop, a candy kitchen and saloons.

Mark Twain's Cabin is a short distance north of Columbia. Indian Grinding Rock State Park is full of Indian lore galore. Overnight at Mine Inn, Amador City, and a performance of the Claypipers at Drytown Theatre is a treat. A rollicking melodrama of the Old West, complete with a villain to boo, a damsel in distress and a chorus line between acts; it shouldn't be missed.

Picnic at Marshall Gold Discovery Park in Coloma. Nevada City and Grass Valley are lovely towns at the northern end of Highway 49.

We stay at National Hotel, 156-years-old, and go on a walking tour of Nevada City, a town with great old buildings, exquisite shops and even a wine tasting room. We ended our trip with a visit to the Empire Mine State Park. The grounds are beautiful. Tour the Bourne Mansion as well as the mine.

Submitted by Beth Thomas

TULE LAKE

The Tule Lake Area, in my eyes, is in one of the most beautiful areas in Northern California. As a high desert plateau in the Klamath Basin, you can see beautiful scenery, view wildlife, take an auto tour, go hiking, camping, canoeing and more.

In winter, five to six hundred eagles migrate to the Tule Lake Area. In fall, this area has one of the greatest concentrations of waterfowl in North America. Over one million geese, ducks and trumpeter swans migrate to the area. In spring and summer, huge numbers of baby birds can be observed. This is a great time to take a canoe trail on Tule Lake. Watch for antelope, deer and coyote on land.

To the East of Tule Lake are the

Trumpeter Swans at Tule Lake.

Petroglyphs. This cliff was sacred to early Native Americans and each carving on the rocks tells a story of their lives. In the many crevices in this cliff you can find hawks, owls, and prairie falcons.

Captain Jack's stronghold and historical area (at the South end of the lake) was the site of a famous battle between army troops and Modoc Indians. Take the self-guided hike. You can also explore lava tubes (some lit), in nearby Lava Beds National Monument. Camping is available here.

To get there, take I-5 North to US 97, right on Highway 161 to Hill Road.

Submitted by Eileen Oram

BURNT RANCH

Fifty-five miles from Arcata or 85 miles from Redding on Highway 299 is Burnt Ranch, a community of about 300 located in the shadow of beautiful Ironside Mountain. On Christmas day 1994 several of the town's residents, as

Hiking at the Trinity River.

well as some out-of-towners, took a lovely, relaxed hike from Highway 299 to the river. We met no one, coming or going, on our route. This area all along the Trinity River is very historic and beautiful. There is good fishing and swimming. Folks still pan for gold as they did in 1849. The names of the towns and communities are interesting: Burnt Ranch (was there really a ranch that burned?) and Hoopa, for the Native Americans of the Hoopa Tribe and Hayfork. Many places have "Bar" as a part of their name—Somes Bar, Hawkins Bar and Big Bar. Closer to Redding is Whiskeytown and Junction City. Weaverville is the county seat.

There can be snow in the winter and the summers are generally hot. Many of the people living in or around Burnt Ranch are there because they wanted to get away from the bustle of the big cities.

My daughter, Kathleen, told me not to mention her name or she might be banished from the community. They do not want to meet anyone on their trails! I continue to have many happy times in Burnt Ranch.

Submitted by Donna Graham

LAKE SHASTA

C I have discovered the activity and location that satisfies every reason for taking a vacation in the first place. Excitement or tranquillity; luxury or back-to-nature adventure; safety, freedom; convenience and oh, did I mention, romance?

What is this excursion into paradise? Houseboating on Lake Shasta! About 200 miles north of the Bay Area, Lake Shasta is a man-made reservoir created by the confluence of several rivers. With hundreds of miles of shoreline and a myriad of landscapes resulting from the flooding of mountain and foothill ravines, it's a never-ending exploration.

As an avid water skier, I live for this setting. Miles of glassy-calm channels, acres of deep, clean, cool, open water and a minimum of those dreaded no wake zones make Lake Shasta a skier's delight. You simply tie your ski boat to the back of the houseboat and take it with you throughout your vacation. From dawn until dusk, you're only seconds away from a water ski run whenever the impulse strikes you.

The houseboat itself is a floating first-class home away from home. They are available in various sizes and come with luxury features such as microwaves and trash compactors. Most are equipped with generators which allow you to operate home appliances you just can't live without, (blenders, hair dryers and VCRs). All have bathrooms (some have two) and kitchens. The boats are fun and relatively simple to operate. There are several locations on the lake that rent houseboats on a daily or weekly basis.

After a day of rigorous skiing, hours of exploration, and non-stop relaxation, it's time for dinner. You can prepare a gourmet meal in the galley, or tie up at one of several resorts and dine at one of their restaurants. Most rental boats are equipped with outside gas grills as well as cooktop stoves and ovens; so it's much more fun and convenient to "stay home" and eat right where you plan to tie up for the night.

And—this may be the best part— the top of the houseboat also serves as a patio and an observation deck! At night, I love to sleep on the roof and take in the splendor of the milky-way and a heaven so full of reach-out-and-touchable stars that there's hardly any room left for sky. You don't have enough fingers and toes to count the shooting stars; and, if there happens to be a full moon...well, you may never return to civilization. After the sun slips below the silhouette of the foothills and forests, the night sounds take over: the gentle rippling of water against the houseboat pontoons, an occasional hoot of an owl, and the light rustling of the deer, only an arms-length away, who have come to see if you just might have forgotten to eat your dessert or part

Houseboating on Lake Shasta

of your salad.

In the morning, it's up at first light to see the sunrise and catch a ripple-free barefoot ski run, back for some bragging and a hearty breakfast of bacon and eggs and maybe a screwdriver or Bloody Mary, some hot coffee and then you start the whole cycle over again.

What a great life!!!

Submitted by Craig Hardman

AA RANCH

As a pilot since the age of 18, I have appreciated the convenience that general aviation has provided millions of Americans. This is especially true for those weekend getaways. One of my favorites is the AA Ranch located in Southern Trinity County near Ruth, California.

Cabins are available, with tents for the more adventurous, and the dining room serves 3 meals daily. There are daily horseback rides and a heated pool to wash off the trail dust at the end of the day. Also tennis and volleyball courts and lots of scenic hiking. The bar has a jukebox for some Country & Western music and dancing.

AA is open May through September. Call 707-574-6227 for more information.

Submitted by Mark D. Lindberg

LASSEN COUNTY

It was quite enjoyable to find that there is a mini-Yellowstone here on Northern California's Mt. Lassen. Hiking in Mt. Lassen is very comfortable. There are wooden boardwalks on some of the trails. The scenery was, quite varied and interesting, and at the end of the trail, a wonderful mix of desolate ground, fascinating formations and bubbling ponds with varying colors and smells.

Of course, there are many other

The majestic view looking down from the trail to the mudpot area at Mt. Lassen.

trails to follow within the park that lead you through beautiful forests, cool streams, gorgeous waterfalls and up to high peaks with great views, as well as very nice, comfortable campgrounds. It's a wonderful place to visit.

Submitted by the Wheelers

My son Nick was home for a visit from the University of Santa Barbara and our trip to Mt. Lassen was a wonderful way for just the two of us to enjoy the time we had together. Our trip took place five years ago; however, we still laugh and talk about it today.

Never before have I had such a struggle or a more breathtaking sight as the glorious moment when I reached the peak of Mt. Lassen. Nick had gone ahead since I was a little slower, but it was fun talking to all the others resting along the way. I thought I would give up several times; but I just kept plugging along until I made it, and I have never been sorry.

From Mt. Lassen's peak, we

could see Mt. Shasta, many lakes and the beautiful valley below. It is one of the most enchanting and diversified parks I have experienced. We also really enjoyed all the nature trails and wildlife. One favorite hike was the Bumpass Hell Nature Trail.

When you are there, plan some time to travel a little farther north and visit

Phyllis at Summit of Mt. Lassen.

McArthur-Burney Falls Memorial State Park where fishing is popular at the base of the falls. Burney Falls is very beautiful and the trails and foliage are very enjoyable. Some scenes from the movie "Willow" were filmed there.

Submitted by Phyllis Krest

Nick at McArthur-Burney Falls.

Driving from Red Bluff, traveling east on Northern California Highway 36, the country gradually changes. Out of the dead flat Sacramento farming valley we climb ever so gently through cattle ranches past a dry lake and suddenly, as if out of nowhere, we are surrounded by volcano country.

Countless acres, as far as the eye can see, are littered with millions of boulders. One can almost imagine a giant hand scattering them like confetti over the landscape.

To the left, Mt. Shasta is visible and covered in snow, the majestic mountain reaches to the heavens. We catch a glimpse of an extinct cinder cone, hundreds of feet tall, poking its head through the terrain.

As we continue on, the countryside becomes covered with scrub oaks and scattered with beasts. Reaching the 2,500-foot elevation point, we are in the midst of a valley formed by monstrous rock formations resembling haphazardly–made layer cakes.

Traveling on through the charming little villages of Dales Station, Paynes Creek, Ponderosa Sky Ranch and up into the thick forest areas, the winding road leads into the hamlet of Mineral, site of the Lassen Volcanic Park Headquarters. This is a mountain valley at 5,000 feet. The road stretches through pine and fir along Highway 89 into Lassen Park. The scene ahead is inviting, yet forbidding, for ahead is Mt. Lassen. A North American live volcano, its snow-capped top disguises the danger brimming below.

This awesome volcano is only a four to five hour drive from San Francisco and is a striking example of Mother Nature's power.

Submitted by Frank McGovern

Frank "Muscles" McGovern carrying the meteorite to Mt. Lassen.

One of my favorite spots in Northern California is a place my family and I have gone to for many vacations, Lassen Volcanic National Park. Our encounter with nature always began at the Black Forest Lodge, a small motel outside the park where we would inevitably stay. The Lodge was plain but clean; all the furniture and appliances seemed preserved from the 1950s - and there was no television. We enjoyed spot ting the many deer in the pasture, looking for falling stars at night, and being awakened by cows right

Alison and family near the Sulfur Works.

outside our door in the morning! Every morning we'd go to the homey restaurant upstairs and order from the same menu that has been there for the last ten years. It was great!

When we weren't nature watching at the motel, Pop would drive us through Lassen Park and watch for the numbered signs on the side of the road which corresponded to

a description in the road guide, which my Mom would read to us. One of the traditional photo stops was at the Sulfur Works, a place that emitted pungent rotting egg fumes. Holding our breath, we'd stand in front of the malodorous cloud and force a smile for the camera before racing back to the car, gasping. We would take several hours to climb up a mountain trail, stopping often to munch on a sandwich, take a picture, or rest our trail-weary legs and take in the pine-scented smell of the forest.

Submitted by Alison Sue

F LAKE PLUMAS

ur family enjoys camping, fishing, swimming, hiking and simply being out in nature. The scenic Feather River Canyon leads

you to one of many great lakes.

Bucks Lake, Mill Creek Campgrounds, is nestled among trees along the lake shore. It offers ten campsites, water, flush toilets, fireplaces and picnic tables. It's only twenty miles from Quincy; no reservations are required.

Antelope Lake, Boulder Creek

The many Geese at Bucks Lake.

Campground, Lone Rock Campground and Long Point Campground all provide camping with lake views. Twenty-four miles from Taylorville on Beckworth

and Indian Creek Road, these lakes offer an abundance of swimming and fishing.

Submitted by Rich Bortolin

G MT. SHASTA

One of my favorite destinations is Mt. Shasta. This area is one of California's best kept secrets. The county is 80 percent national and state lands and offers a tremendous environmental variety from alpine forests to high desert plateaus.

I love this area because it is an outdoor enthusiast's paradise. Both the Klamath National Forest and Shasta-Trinity National Forest are located within Siskiyou County, as well as Lava Beds National Monument.

There are many rivers and lakes including the head waters of the Sacramento River and beautiful Lake Siskiyou. If you like to fish or hike, this is the place to do it. Mt. Shasta is spectacular to behold. Rising over 14,000 feet, this is one of California's largest mountains.

In the winter, I like to ski at Mt. Shasta Ski Park and in the summer my favorite activity is mountain biking in this wondrous setting. There is a company called *Over The Hill Cycling Tours* that offers guided day and multi-day excursions in the area. This is a great way to go. They have a support van to carry your gear and all the food and water, leaving you free to ride. I really like having guides to show me routes that I wouldn't know about otherwise, and it's fun to ride with a group! The multi-day tours are really a blast and I would highly recommend this activity to other biking enthusiasts.

Mt. Shasta has several bed-and-breakfast inns in addition to motels; but my favorite is a retreat called Stewart Mineral Springs that is located in Parks Creek Canyon, a town north of a little canyon. You can rent a small cabin or even stay in a teepee beside Parks Creek, a beautiful mountain stream. They offer mineral baths that are a must!

There are many good restaurants, cute shops and art galleries to visit in this darling little town. I recommend Bellisimo or Lilly's for dining and advise you to checkout the Black Bear Gallery. The Mt. Shasta Resort, just outside of a town near Lake Siskiyou, has excellent dining, golfing, tennis and wonderful accommodations.

Contact the Siskiyou County Visitors Bureau or the Mt. Shasta Chamber of Commerce for more information.

Submitted by
Barbara Ulrich Schiff

EASTERN SHASTA

We live in Eastern Shasta County. It is a picnicker's paradise. Some travelers favorite spots are beside Hat Creek on Highway 44-89.

Catch a trout while you are there, if you like. Manzanita Lake near the entrance of Lassen National Park is another beauty spot. Off Highway 44 - East on Highway 89 to Burney Falls State Park.

There are lots of picnic tables and fireplaces in the forest or beside Lake Britton. Early fall and late spring it is uncrowded and quite beautiful, with outside activities such as boating, swimming, fishing and hiking.

This corner of California is not crowded and offers magnificent vistas plus a variety of things to do. There is also an abundance of lovely birds and animals, too.

Submitted by W. L. Johnson

SISKIYOU

Our favorite getaway spot is our cabin in the woods. It is located 17 miles east of McCloud, in Siskiyou County. The cabin is surrounded by trees. A railroad track runs along side and a work train runs daily. We're only five miles from the beautiful McCloud River, where rainbow trout add to fishing enjoyment.

We enjoy the quiet and peaceful atmosphere, but we also enjoy people. So to anyone driving on Hwy East 89, take the Medicine Lake turn to Harris Spring Road. Stop and say "hi," our cabin is about 3/4 miles in.

Submitted by Al & Peg Franklin

Rustic and peaceful Bartel Cabin near McCloud.

HIGH SIERRA

SILVER LAKE

I have traveled all over California and nothing compares to the peace and tranquillity I have experienced at Kit Carson Lodge. Nestled in the foothills overlooking Silver Lake, the lodge is a wonderful place to center myself and become one with nature. It is a place for peace. During the day, I spend my time climbing rocks and taking pictures in the area just west of the lake. There is a rushing river, wonderful glacial rock and no people. Just me and the sound of rushing water.

At sunset, I go to the edge of the lake and listen to the skies pulse with thunder as Thunder Mountain contracts in the cool of the evening. Then, after the sun goes down, I sit at the edge of the

Jennifer relaxing at Silver Lake.

dock and listen to the ducks call one another as they come to the lake. Finally, as darkness falls, I look to the sky and become absorbed by the vast star show above.

I hear the lake lapping at the dock. I see more than my mind can absorb. And I know where my place is in the world. I am at peace.

Submitted by Jennifer Carole

Silver Lake is the kind of place you stumble upon accidentally. It is like a dream that happens amid the skiing, boating, gambling and other recreation you normally find in the Sierra Nevada mountains. Peaceful, serene, undisturbed and inviting.

The unending beauty is its silent wonder. There aren't four separate seasons at Silver Lake. It is a single season of change. The snowy mountain tops, the half-frozen lake, the warm breezes through the pines and the rolling

meadows all meet together in a place you can only call nature.

While at Silver Lake, it is nature that provides the recreation. A beautiful campground is located

David stops for photo at Silver Lake.

at the foot of the lake. Horse and hiking trails are everywhere around the area. Nearby are Carson Pass at 8,650 feet, Twin

Lakes and the Pacific Crest National Scenic Trail. Even the restaurant located on the lake offers spectacular views of the area and the adjacent horse ranch.

There are few places left where nature has been allowed to remain in control, changing simply, innocently and freely. Silver Lake is one of them. I hope you enjoy it as I have.

Submitted by David W. Anderson

B YOSEMITE

Although I have lived in California since 1956, I had never taken a trip to Yosemite National Park until 1985. I signed up for a two-day photography workshop so I could learn about the park. Since then, I have been going back at least once a year for the past 10 years.

One of my favorite hikes is the Upper Yosemite Falls Trail. It's about 3 1/2 miles from the trailhead at Sunnyside Campground to the top of Yosemite Falls. The roundtrip takes about 6-8 hours.

The photograph of me is at Columbia Rock, about a mile up the trail, where you get an excellent view of Half Dome. This trail was built in 1873 and leads to the world's third highest waterfall. It is 2,425 feet from the valley floor. You need to bring enough water

Betty at the upper Yosemite Falls trail.

as this is rated a strenuous hike since you have a 2,700-foot elevation gain and it's often quite warm.

You know that you have accomplished some thing when you reach the top!

Submitted by Betty Molloy

C SORENSON'S

Are you looking for the perfect place for a family adventure, business conference or romantic getaway? Well, you've found it! Sorensen's is a beautiful year-round resort. It's located at 14255 Highway 88 in Hope Valley.

Sorensen's is a mom and pop business. It has a cozy cafe where you can go inside and eat, play a game, or sip your complimentary hot drink. There are over 20 secluded log cabins. Some sleep up to eight people. The uniquely named cabins all have kitchens; some also have lofts. There is a sauna among the cabins, and many sledding trails between the trees.

The snow is magnificent!

There are many cross country ski trails at the site. Kirkwood Ski Resort is only 20 miles away!

At Sorensen's neither kids nor parents will get bored. Many activities are offered: painting, music, hiking, biking, fishing, skiing and other sports, crafts, wreath making and even star gazing.

I've only been fortunate enough to visit Sorensen's during the winter; but I'm sure it's as good or better in the summer...but that's up to you to find out!

Submitted by Shannon Griggs

Sorenson's Resort

45

HIGH SIERRA

SIERRA REGION

September is a time to start planning an escape to see the aspens, maples and oaks which will be

Rock Creek in the fall at Inyo National Forest.

changing colors and dropping their leaves for winter. My travel plans are often influenced by regional guests who appear on John Hamilton's Saturday morning program. They are the best sources for current information on timing and location of fall color.

The Eastern Sierra is magnificent in October when aspens blanket hillsides and flow down canyon walls in great washes of gold. Rabbitbrush, blooming yellow, provides a perfect foreground. Happy fishermen can be found in the creeks.

Either of the following trips can be an ambitious weekend excursion, or combine them, if time allows, four to six days for leisurely exploration.

Start in Jackson and take Highway 88 East, past Silver Lake and over Carson pass, through Hope Valley, where there is lodging at Sorensen's and fabulous camping at Blue Lakes, to Highway 89 South. Pass through Markleeville (food and lodging are available) and then go up to Monarch Pass. If this is a weekend trip, turn around here and then take Highway 4 West to Angels Camp and home.

Trip number two: Take Highway 120 East through Yosemite to Highway 395 and turn south toward Mammoth Lakes, where you can take side trips to Mono Lake and June Lake Loop. The turn around point of this journey is Bishop; but be sure to visit Convict Lake, Rock Creek, South Lake and Sabrina Lake (both west of Bishop). Return home through Yosemite or by Highway 108 over Sonora Pass, if you want different views on your return trip.

Each year in October, Lone Pine, at the foot of Mt. Whitney and home to many movie set locations, hosts a film festival and features appearances by western film stars.

There are plenty of campgrounds and motels along this route; so feel free to dawdle here and there, enjoy the warm sun and cool air, revel in the intense aspen colors, and bed down at the nearest home-away-from-home location. The Eastern Sierra is beautiful and dramatic; the locals are friendly and helpful.

Submitted by Diana Petersen

You don't have to go to New England States to find autumn color when we have it right here in California. After the first few frosts hit the mountains of the Sierra Range, take Highway 88 NE out of Stockton towards the Gold country via Jackson. Continue on 88 over Carson Pass towards Kirkwood ski area. You pass by two of the most beautiful lakes in Northern California, Silver Lake and Caples.

That's where the color really begins. Drop down after Carson Pass into 7000' Hope Valley and the mountains are alive with brilliant golds and tinges of red and still a bit

South Lake in Eastern Sierra in the fall.

of green.

Stay on Highway 88 on past the Junction of 88 and 89 and you come to Sorensen's Resort, a quaint Norwegian restaurant and cabin resort. Another six miles and you arrive at Woodfords Junction. Turn right at the flashing yellow light and seven miles farther on 89 puts you into to the village of Woodfords, County seat of Alpine County. A village reminiscent of the Vermont landscape. Turn right at the Cutthroat Saloon and go 3 miles west to Grover Hot Springs State Park. There you can soak in the 104 degree natural waters and cool down in the cold pool adjacent to it.

It's worth the trip and just under 200 miles from the Bay Area.

Submitted by Jewell Bethel

Welcome to Bridgeport, California, with a population of 700. It is in Mono County and one of the most beautiful places in California and one of its best-kept secrets. The town is located in a small, lush valley surrounded by high mountains with an elevation of 6400 feet.

It has many lakes full of large brown trout. Twin Lakes boasts great fishing and spectacular scenery. Robinson Creek, Buckeye Creek, Virginia Lakes, Green Creek and Green Lake are other places within 15 minutes from town where you can catch any kind of trout you can eat.

There is something for everyone in or near Bridgeport. It's only a short drive to Hawthorne, Nevada, for gambling and nighttime fun. Bridgeport even has its own ghost town nearby, named Bodie.

There are many hiking trails and plenty of places to go mountain climbing on the Matterhorn of the Sawtooth Ridge.

Bridgeport puts on a genuine old-fashioned Fourth of July complete with a parade and barbecue, games such as nail driving, greased pole and tug-of-war, and an incredible fireworks display cap off this annual event.

Come to Bridgeport for a day, you're bound to spend another.

Submitted by Benno Huene

CENTRAL COAST

MONTEREY

The most beautiful walk or bicycle ride along the Pacific Coast starts near the Monterey Bay Aquarium and takes you to Asilomar Beach in Pacific Grove.

Where else can you walk or ride by stately Victorian houses on one side and peer into interesting tide pools or watch crashing breakers on the other? You can stop off at any of the little coves or beaches on the way or take time to climb the rocks

on Lover's Point, or rest awhile on the sandy Pacific Grove beach. As you walk along the edge of the bay until it meets the ocean, you can admire seals and sea gulls sunning on the rocks, or watch sea otters cracking open their dinner while floating on their backs. Prehistoric looking pelicans fly by in single file, skimming the water. In the winter, you may even be lucky enough to see whales spouting as they swim down the coast toward the warm waters of Baja.

A walk in the evening watching a sunset can often be spectacular, and watching a full moon rise over the bay can be an unforgettable sight. This easy, level three mile trip is one you will long remember.

Submitted by
Doris Barnard Bragdon

You may have heard of Monterey Bay or maybe the cities around it such as Santa Cruz, Monterey, Carmel and Capitola; but few tourists hear about how to experience the Bay itself. It offers incredible wildlife, a means of recreation such as surfing, sailing, scuba diving and kayaking, beautiful beaches and, of course, a lovely thing to look at while relaxing.

One of my favorite ways to experience Monterey Bay is through

ON THE GO WITH KGO RADIO

whale watching. Many whale watching expeditions leave from the Fisherman's Wharf in Monterey. It is there that you board a medium sized fishing boat and head out onto the bay for two to three hours. I can tell you from experience that there is nothing in the world like seeing graceful gray whales come out of the water less than ten feet away from you; but beware, it will spoil Marine World forever.

I recommend Randy's Fishing Trips. For more information call 408-372-0577.

Submitted by Greta Hansen

My favorite getaway place for a few days is Pacific Grove. I like its slower pace and more relaxed atmosphere versus living in a large, hectic city in the San Francisco Bay Area.

I like to walk, and the coast there is such a beautiful area. There is a lot to see and do on the Monterey Peninsula. I like to look at the Victorian houses — they are such majestic old buildings. The small Victorians are so cozy looking.

I check the Butterfly Trees to see how many Monarch Butterflies are there each year. At my favorite bed-and-breakfast, the owner's lovely calico cat, Mouse, sleeps on my bed. I come back to San Francisco refreshed from a weekend in "Butterfly Town." It's a really nice place to visit.
Submitted by Laura Herrgott

A docent-guided visit to poet Robinson Jeffer's Tor House, Hawk Tower and old-world garden in Carmel is one of my favorite getaways.

With the guidance of enthusiastic and knowledgeable docents, the love story of Robin and Una Jeffers comes vividly to life amid one of the most charming settings in all of Northern California. Swing open the garden gate; walk among the flowers; explore the enchanted stone cottage; ascend Hawk Tower, built of native granite by Jeffers as a gift for Una; and from its top survey one of the most breathtaking views in the world. Throughout

Above: Oceanview Ave. near Lover's Point.
Right: "Mouse" the owner's cat at a B&B.

the tour the docent showers you with rich detail and reads appropriate selections from Jeffer's poetry. The whole experience temporarily transports you back to what seems to have been a better world.

Tor House is located on Carmel Point, just south of Carmel Village on Ocean View Avenue between Scenic Road and Stewart Way. Carmel is about a two-and-a-half hour drive south of San Francisco on Highway 1, approximately 5 miles south of Monterey.

Tours are conducted on the hour every Friday and Saturday from 10 a.m. through 4 p.m. You must call ahead to reserve a date and time; but, don't hesitate to call the same day, you may get lucky. The number of people on each tour is limited to six. For reservations call (408) 624-1813.

Plan on devoting a couple of hours to this delightful experience and leave children younger than teenagers with a babysitter. You, the children and the others on the tour will be happier.

Jeffer's poetry and books about him and Tor House are on sale at the tour site. If you haven't read

CENTRAL COAST

Jeffer's powerful and evocative poetry, you will want to after coming

Tor House in Carmel.

under the spell of his stone poems, Tor House and Hawk Tower.

Submitted by Wes & Jennie George

The Mission Ranch, located right behind the Mission in Carmel, is a place I would recommend to anyone. If you are lucky enough to visit the ranch for more than just lunch, brunch or dinner, you are fortunate. It has the most serene setting and is among the few really tranquil places I have visited. We have stayed in the Mission on two occasions. The rooms and suites are very comfortable, with big fluffy beds and lots of pillows and comforters. Some of the rooms have wood stoves or whirlpools; ours didn't, but the setting is so great it didn't matter. If you are really lucky, you get to see the owner, Clint Eastwood.

If you only have one day for a trip, try to make it Sunday because the restaurant has the most wonderful brunch. You have the choice of sitting on the outdoor terrace, which has a terrific view of the bay and is located above a pasture, where you can view the horses and sheep. The second choice for seating is inside the renovated western style area. There are three fireplaces and windows are everywhere. There is also a jazz combo every Sunday.

Banquet table on patio barn at Mission Ranch.

The location is right off of Highway 1 in Carmel. Turn on Rio Road past the Mission - watch for the Mission Ranch sign.

Submitted by Judy T. DeVilbiss

BIG SUR

This area is on California's coast, one hour south of Monterey. There are plenty of trails for good hiking where you may find creeks or even hot springs to relax in. I highly recommend Big Sur and its beautiful scenery.

Rustic Deetien's Big Sur Inn is a very homey group of board and batten shacks that resemble a shipwreck. It is listed on the National Registry of Historical places and, therefore, its structure can not be altered. It is a non-profit organization run by a preservation foundation. The rooms are $70-$135. Fifteen out of twenty of them have their own bathroom. There are fireplaces in many of the rooms and a unique collection of books.

There is an esalen institute that features natural hot springs. This is a conference center. You need to call about one week in advance to make a reservation. If the seminar is not full, there may be room for boarders. Boarders pay about $150 a night for three delicious vegetarian meals and use of the hot springs. The hot springs are on the cliff overlooking the ocean. I highly recommend them!

After a weekend in Big Sur you feel relaxed because you can get away from the hurried life of the city. It is not commercial. There is a quietness and a beauty of nature in this great experience.

Submitted by Jacob Huskey

SAN JUAN BAUTISTA

Just over two hours from San Francisco, San Juan Bautista is a well-preserved example of life in a simpler time. A historic walking tour of the tiny town reveals its early California roots. The leisurely stroll winds through Mission San Juan Bautista, city gardens and several charming restaurants, an-

Mission San Juan Bautista

tique stores, art galleries and specialty shops, many housed in original wood or adobe buildings which date back to the early 1800s.

Gazing down the town's main thoroughfare, where the only traffic is a rooster leading his harem of hens across the street, it's easy to imagine a troop of Mexican soldiers marching in step under the blazing California sun while the mission bell tolls in the distance.

Though the town depends on tourism, there are no fast food restaurants or gaudy neon signs. The approximately 1,600 residents take great pride in maintaining the historic nature of their town. Merchants dress in full period costumes the first Saturday of each month.

This is a wonderful spot for a family outing, a leisurely lunch or a special romantic weekend. The town hosts several annual festivals and events throughout the year, including perfor-

mances by El Teatro Campesino, a nationally known theater group.

Submitted by Charles Steligo

This sleepy, authentic wayside of American/Spanish history, is only two miles off of Highway 101, located almost exactly half way between 156 East Carmel and Santa Cruz.

There are many restaurants to tempt a visitor—including one for earthquake aficionados called "The Faultline" which is exactly what you are dining on. Jardines (pronouced Hardines) De San Juan Garden restaurant, may feature mariachis playing at a wedding reception in one corner of the large patio—or some other kind of live music, an original recipe for margaritas, and south of the border fare. Delightful. A lovely new hotel in the heart of town, Posada De San Juan Hotel, has a massive lobby, fireplaces in artfully decorated rooms and reasonable rates; and is only a few steps from

another old-time favorite restaurant, The Mariposa, which features a celebrated woman chef.

Antique shops, specialty stores and, of course, the Old Mission will beckon.

For a feeling of being back-in-time—a calmer, sweeter time—treat yourself to this jewel of California Spanish history. An events calendar is available at the Chamber of Commerce, located on 3rd Street of the small downtown between Polk and Muckelemi streets. Every year there is a flea market in August and a Peddler's Fair in June which are magnets to faithful collectors and browsers from everywhere!

Submitted by Shirley Parks

There's natural beauty all-around Big Sur.

THE BAY AREA

EAST BAY

California's East Bay Area is known for its mild climate, beautiful waterways, variety of activities and rich history. Jack London Square, located in Oakland, weaves all these

Dorothy enjoys the wharf at Jack London Square.

attractions into a fun place to explore. It contains more than twenty unique shops, several excellent restaurants, a museum, Jack London's log cabin, and "Heinold's First and Last Chance Saloon," frequented by such famous people as President William Howard Taft, Robert Louis Stevenson and Joaquin Miller. It was where Jack London studied as a child and later wrote notes for some of his books. Visiting the saloon is like stepping back in time. Most of the original furnishings are in use today.

Barnes and Noble Bookstore is quite popular. Its 150,000 titles, spacious, bright areas, comfortable chairs and tables, upstairs cafe with a view, gourmet coffee, tea, and pastries create the perfect environment for treasure hunting.

People come to shop, eat, relax in the sun, watch the boats on the water, and enjoy the peaceful tune of the shore.

Viewing one of the waterfront's spectacular watermelon sunsets is an unforgettable way to end the day.

Submitted by Dorothy E. Dorsey

There are quite a few places one can go to see nature. However, there is only one place where you can see what kind of plants lived in the Bay Area before people and their imported plants arrived. That place is the Botanic Garden in Berkeley's Tilden Park.

The entire garden contains nothing but native California plants. You will not find Chinese azaleas, Australian eucalyptus trees or French herbs.

See California's rich botanic legacy before it is too late and the imported "weeds" take over. Discover shrubs, flowers and grasses found nowhere else in the world. Many are rare or endangered.

Submitted by Jerry Hashimoto

To visit Old Town Benicia is to take a step back into the history of the 1850s. It is a place where your imagination can soar, where there is peace and beauty on a hillside with many dreams.

Imagine! A town that was the state Capitol for only thirteen months. Ferries once transported as many as 26 transcontinental railroad cars at one time from their port. Many historical buildings and churches were the first of their kind in all of California, and camels once transported the Military Arsenal, which served the area for 100 years. One house was built in Boston and shipped around the Horn and reassembled.

Today, old buildings house antique shops, arts and crafts by local artists and restaurants.

Down side streets one can find flowering trees surrounding pioneer homes, well-preserved Victorian homes, and a low, rambling house where dangling flower pots over a porch with old wicker chairs speak of a slower pace of living.

The City Park and benches throughout the town invite you to pause, rest, enjoy and dream– dream of what was and where so much of California "living" and history began.

Submitted by Anne Peterson

I love roses, so I like to go to the Berkeley Rose Garden. It's a heavenly place to be when the roses are in full bloom and their sweet fragrances permeate the air.

The blooming period extends from late spring to early fall.

Rose lovers should bring their journals to jot down different varieties, since all of the roses are labeled. Bush, tree and climbing roses will be a delight to gardeners' eyes.

Photographers should be prepared to shoot at least a roll of film, because there are so many beautiful rose specimens, not to speak of the great aerial shots of the rose terraces and the East Bay you can take from the entrance.

Plan to go during the week, if you wish to meditate during the quiet afternoon

hours. On weekends, after brunch, take a short stroll along the paths and terraces. There are benches to sit on to catch your breath and visit a while with friends.

Open every day from dawn to dusk, the Berkeley Rose Garden is located in the 1400 block of Euclid Avenue in Berkeley.

Submitted by Janet Fox

Almost every Saturday at 8 a.m., in any weather, I look forward to meeting with a friendly assortment of people at Oakland's Lake Merritt Spanish-style Old Boat

More Great Places To Go From KGO...

House, across the street from the imposing Scottish Rite Temple and beside the restored Cameron-Stanford Victorian home.

This is the East Bay chapter of the

Left: Anne Peterson in front of the Riddell-Fish House, a Queen Anne Victorian in Benecia.
Above: Roses are in full bloom at the Berkeley Rose garden.

THE BAY AREA

Golden Gate Race Walkers. As a member for more than seven years, I have weekly race-walked the 3.1-mile route around the lake and its

A few of the Golden Gate Race Walkers.

constantly changing vistas. This beautiful saltwater lake is a refuge for many birds. During these Saturday walks I may see several types of herons, pelicans, ducks and large flocks of Canadian geese, who try to ignore the passing humans while wary squirrels decide which way to dart.

Also out on Saturdays are joggers, bicyclists, Tai-Chi practitioners, lawnbowling enthusiasts and crew teams, oars in unison, skimming over the lake.

Lake Merritt, with its Grecian columns at one end, an old-fashioned bandstand, plus its proximity to the Oakland Museum and BART, is truly an urban gem. Coupled with the fun of participating with a congenial walking group, the lake is an ideal destination.

Submitted by Pam Webb

NORTH BAY

My favorite place to visit is the Point Reyes area. It's great to go hiking, swimming in Tomales Bay, browsing in the shops in Inverness, and, oh yeah, celebrating my birthday. My friend Rembert and I recently celebrated my birthday there.

I also like the town of Parkfield.

The scenery, cafe and the Inn make this place a good weekend getaway. The road from Highway 198 is neat. Very scenic. I visit Parkfield often.

Submitted by Steve Freschl

Crashing surf, soaring hawks, serene lakes, cascading brooks, spectacular vistas. In the spring, a thunderous waterfall. The Coastal Trail from the Palomarin Trailhead to Wildcat Camp, and a side trip to Alamere Falls. The Point Reyes National Seashore has it all.

The hike, including Alamere Falls, is 13 miles round trip; however, there is little change in elevation and hikers can turn around at any point to accommodate the time and energy of the group. Bring food and water. The trip is best taken in the winter or spring when the falls and meandering streams are at their fullest. Fog and heavy winds are often prevalent during summer.

To find the Palomarin Trailhead, take the Bolinas (unmarked) turn-off from Highway 1, just north of Stinson Beach. Turn right at Mesa Road and drive about 4 miles to the Point Reyes Bird Observatory. From there follow the unpaved road another mile to the trailhead parking lot.

The trail begins in a eucalyptus grove and continues through scrub brush before emerging on a bluff

An awesome shot of the Alamere Falls.

300 feet above the pounding Pacific, with views of the Farallon Islands and even of San Francisco to the south. Later, the trail turns inland and crosses through more

mountainous terrain. Soon, the trail passes small ponds and begins following creeks before opening up to beautiful Bass Lake, and, further on, peaceful Pelican Lake perched above the Pacific. From there you can see Chimney Rock and Point Reyes Lighthouse to the north. An unmarked and unofficial trail to the west, just beyond this point, leads to an overlook of Alamere Creek and Falls.

The main trail continues past Ocean and Wildcat Lakes and into Wildcat Camp. After a well-deserved lunch, hike south along the beach to see Alamere Falls as it cascades over sea cliffs onto the beach and out to sea.

Submitted by
Suzy & Stone Coxhead

My husband and I have two young daughters who love to camp. Being longtime San Francisco residents, we've tried every nearby campground. China Camp and China Beach Campground in Marin County have won our hearts.

Going north on Highway 101 across the Golden Gate Bridge and about two miles east of Terra Linda, you'll find a slice of the past. California history, fishing, hiking, a great beach and a little brown campground all are what make China Beach wonderful.

China Camp was founded about the time of the Gold Rush by Chinese fishermen fishing for shrimp. A charming pier houses a bait shop, small cafe and a wonderful little museum. Fishing is allowed from the pier, and great hikes for parents and children are everywhere.

We went to China Beach with a group of about 30 campfire girls and boys, and we were treated to a wonderful evening: a flashlight nature walk and a campfire history talk by a pair of friendly rangers.

The next morning we hiked out to Turtle Back Island through low tide and were able to share an educational tide pool experience with the kids.

Parking is easy, the campgrounds have water and fire pits, and you're 45 minutes from downtown San Francisco. Who could ask for more? Spaces are first-come, first-served, so come early Friday afternoons for a good space.

Submitted by Amy Levine

Driving north from San Francisco across the Golden Gate Bridge, you discover a beautiful small town on the bay with a definite Mediterranean quality. This is Sausalito, recognized all over the world because many films have been shot here, and famous and infamous personalities have made this lovely place their home.

Sausalito is loved by tour-

Top: Suzy Coxhead enjoying the surroundings near Pelican Lake.

Middle: The town of Parkfield - and all its fun and glory.

Bottom: Go hiking and camping at China Camp.

ists and natives alike. The citizens are as diverse as the weather. So many activities abound that cater to

Fishing on the Bay on the Salty Lady.

everyone's tastes - from the elegant hotels on the hill where San Franciscans come for a change of pace to the enormous Flea Market that is held on weekends where a visitor may purchase just about anything.

At the foot of Harbor Drive you will find Caruso's, where you can make arrangements to go out sport fishing. They have daily trips. My favorite captain is Roger Thomas,

who has the 60-foot Salty Lady. He knows the surrounding waters like the back of his hand; and, at certain times of the year, he takes parties whale-watching for the Oceanic Club.

Sausalito is just off Highway 101. It is served by the Golden Gate Transit service and also the popular ferry from San Francisco.

***Submitted by
Marie Antonucci***

C PENINSULA

One of the places that our family likes to go to is Memorial Park. It is nestled in the redwood trees near Loma Mar. Memorial Park has great campgrounds with redwood trees that you can climb on and walk through. There is a lot of wildlife.

You can go swimming in the swimming hole and there are lots of hiking trails. You can go backpacking and mountain-biking.

It is just a short distance to

*Mary, Heather and Karissa
in the tree at Memorial Park.*

Pescadero Marsh, where you can hike or go bird-watching. The beach is just a short walk away for sunbathing and whale-watching. On the way back to camp you can stop at some of the farms and pick an evening snack. It is a fun place for the whole family.

Submitted by Patterson Family

I can hardly express my enthusiasm for Filoli in 200 words, because I have spent so much time there as a member/volunteer during my 10 retirement years. After a lifetime of employment, people asked what I was going to do. On a whim I said, "I'm going to join Filoli and become a volunteer." This decision led to a real commitment, and, at times, almost an obsession.

Although I never became a full docent, I have been a hostess on self-guided tour days, have worked on hospitality for special events, and have done quite a bit of work on membership and mailing.

The small annual membership fee of $25 ($20 for seniors) is a modest price to pay for the hours of pleasure one can derive from frequent visits to the wonderful gardens. Plus, with all the special events and the nature hikes in the undeveloped portion of the property, it just can't be beat.

Submitted by Ethel Lapuyade

The Allied Arts Guild in Menlo Park is just a few blocks north of the Stanford Shopping Center.

The Allied Arts Guild is a place known to generations of locals. The lovely and serene gardens and comfortable Spanish architecture make this place a peaceful oasis in our pell-mell world. (Not to be confused with The Oasis just a few blocks away - the famous hangout for generations of Stanford students.)

Drop-in and relax at the Allied Arts Guild.

Visits to the Guild have become a tradition for generations of local residents, including many promi-

nent Peninsula families.

This wonderful, secluded cluster of shops, fountains, gardens and restaurants is maintained to benefit the Children's Hospital at Stanford.

Submitted by Christina Cosme

D SOUTH BAY

Wilder Ranch is a state park just outside of Santa Cruz on Highway 1. As long as you like the outdoors, there is something there for everyone.

For people who like to walk, there is a nature trail along the cliffs overlooking the ocean. Along the way you can see many types of birds and sea otters.

For more serious hikers, or bike riders, there are miles of trails through river ravines and fields.

The most well known part of Wilder Ranch is the group of Victorian houses. Some of the houses have old furniture in them, and you can get a guide to show you throughbirds and sea otters.

There is also a picnic area where you can eat lunch, and for only $6, you can spend the entire day there.

Submitted by Angela Hardy

This may never have occurred to you, but visiting some people's back yards may be quite an interesting experience, especially if you like koi, water gardens and beautiful landscaping. Once a year, in June, the Santa Clara Valley Koi and Water Garden Club (nicknamed the "Fish and Chips Club") sponsors a pond tour in which the public is invited (for a small fee) to visit six of its members' ponds. Most often the ponds are set in the context of some lovely landscaping, which may include waterfalls, gazebos, Japanese topiary, and bridges.

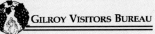

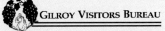

The koi themselves, sometimes called "jewels of the garden," are magnificent to observe. Their graceful movements impart a calmness to the observer and their variety of col-

Observing fish at Santa Clara Koi and Garden.

ors are like a kaleidoscope in the water. The sounds of the waterfalls make hot summer days seem cooler, too.

Every visitor gets a package of informational material about the ponds to be visited, and the hosts are more than eager to go into further detail about technical matters such as filtration systems, pond con-

struction, koi keeping and any questions you may have about water gardens. Each visitor also gets a map of the six pond sites, and may visit them in any sequence they please.

Many past visitors contemplated constructing a pond in their own back yard, and the tour provides a unique source of encouragement and guidance in initiating such an endeavor. Children are especially fascinated watching pond life and get really excited about the prospect of having one in their own backyard.

During the pond tour, children must be closely supervised for safety.

Submitted by Daniel Jacob

Every year, when the children go back to school, I look forward

to their field trip to the Johnson Home and Farm. The Johnson family open its pumpkin patch for autumn jack-o-lantern picking. A hayride is part of the fun. The children all leave with a smile on their faces and a pumpkin perfect for carving. The Johnson Home and Farm is located in Boulder Creek, off Highway 9 about twenty min-

Hayrides and family fun at the Johnson Ranch.

utes north of Santa Cruz. The farm is nestled in the mountains surrounded by a grove of Christmas trees (offered for sale at Christmas time). Adjacent to the farm is a gift shop, picnic area, playground and petting zoo. You can't miss this

delightful experience.

Submitted by Susan Waltz

SAN FRANCISCO

My favorite luxurious getaway lasts only three-and-a-half hours and is right in the heart of San Francisco. It's the Sunday Jazz Brunch at The Ritz-Carlton Hotel on Nob Hill.

This extraordinary buffet brunch is served every Sunday from 11 a.m. to 2:30 p.m. in the Ritz's Terrace dining room.

Once you are seated, a member of the dining room staff will greet you and personally take you on a tour of the buffet stations that are positioned in the foyer and in the main dining room. Then you are on your own to indulge to your heart's content. There is a caviar table with three varieties of caviar that can be enjoyed with freshly-made blinis and assorted toppings. Smoked salmon, oysters on the half shell, large gulf shrimp and made-to-your-order sushi are some of the other seafood offerings. Hot entree selections usually include a succulent rack of lamb, a cooked-to-perfection veal roast and a creative pasta dish. There is an array of sea-

Sunday brunch at the Ritz-Carlton with (l-r): Beverly Dubrin, Paul Nanes and James Dubrin.

sonal salads, fresh fruits and vegetables, cheeses, and delectable muffins, breads and breakfast pastries. While "traditional" brunch items are not the main focus of

brunch at The Ritz, homemade blintzes, eggs benedict or florentine, breakfast meats, and other breakfast selections are always included and are always delicious. Desserts, including miniature French pastries, cakes, and tortes, are temptingly displayed on a large table in the main dining room. Orange juice and coffee are included with the meal and poured continuously.

On sunny days, I prefer to dine al fresco on The Terrace's sunny, flower-filled garden courtyard. Regardless of the weather, there is always seating in the pleasant indoor dining room that overlooks the courtyard.

Live music by the Ritz-Carlton Jazz Quintet entices me to arrive early, dine leisurely, and to stay until the last notes of music are played. The price for this indulgent afternoon of food and music? It's $38 for adults, $19

for children. Reservations are advised and can be made by calling 415-296-7465.

Submitted by Beverly Dubrin

San Francisco is my city, your city, everyone's city. It is my favorite place to live and spend my leisure hours. There is something here to "whet the appetite" of world travelers and stays-at-home alike. Among my favorite spots is the Chevron Corporation's "A Garden in the City" near Second and Market Streets, which was established in 1965. The garden brings together flowers from all over the world and the arrangements are changed every six weeks to offer a rainbow of colors to attract each passerby's sense for the beautiful.

Another best love is the Promenade at the Golden Gate Bridge Park, where various memorial

bricks are embedded in the pathway. A brick with my name on it was a gift in 1988 for my appearance in the movie "The Right Stuff." I have visitation rights to it, enabling

Baron's "brick" on the Promenade of the Golden Gate Bridge Park.

me to enjoy the fabulous arrays of colors of the foliage year round, plus the gorgeous view of the Golden Gate Bridge fog around its structures. This gift brick inspired me to give a brick to my grand nieces and nephews as a Christmas present in 1988, a gift they cherish to this day; and I also gave a brick as a birthday gift to my friend Chris in Los Angeles the same year. Chris and his wife love our wonderful city and

THE BAY AREA

make a pilgrimage to the Promenade each visit.

Submitted by
Baron von Heisterkampf

A fun-filled day at the San Francisco Zoo delights young and old alike. If you haven't been there for awhile, you'll be pleasantly surprised to see new animals, exhibits and renovations.

It's all happening at the San Francisco Zoo.

Surrounding the displays are gardens filled with flowers, wild birds and butterflies.

There's a special excitement when the lion roars or the elephant trumpets. Few visitors can resist smiling when the mother gorilla cuddles her wiggly off-spring. River otters bring laughter, too, as they clown around and chase fish in their new pool. Photo opportunities of the bald eagles on their wooded island are fantastic as well. Whether it's a tiger or a koala you want to see, the San Francisco Zoo is sure to please.

For an added bonus, visitors might consider joining the San Francisco Zoological Society. Not only will this membership admit you to unlimited visits throughout the year, but it will also entitle you to special programs, night tours and best of all, entrance to 110 other zoos and aquariums throughout California and North America.

For year-round fun, take a walk on the wild side at the San Francisco Zoo.

Submitted by Sandy Cortright

There is a wonderful tour guide in San Francisco, and her name is Grace Ann Walden. She conducts a great tour of the North Beach neighborhood, and she really knows the history of the area.

She goes over the history of the Italian people and why they came to San Francisco. She visits the main church, Saints Peter and Paul, and then goes to a handful of specialty shops that make cheese, sausages and baked bread.

My guests have seen the bread going into brick ovens and tasted new cheeses and pastry. The tour cost is $35 and includes lunch.

The tours are available on Saturdays and during the week. Her phone number is 415-397-8530. I have taken two different groups of relatives on this tour, and they thoroughly enjoyed it.

Submitted by Tracy Shaffer

Top: Ft. Point and the world-famous Golden Gate Bridge.

Left: A bagpiper at the Highland Games in Pleasanton.

Photos by: Diana Petersen

KGO Radio Personalities & Others...

Leo Ciolino

KGO Radio Weatherman

I'm easy to please. I find beauty everywhere, and at any time of the day. I am enamored by the day's first light, and I feel fortunate that I'm awake when nature puts on one of its most awesome displays of beauty: sunrise.

The sky is part of my working equipment. No sunrise or sunset ever captures the thrills of the previous one. Each has a magnetism of its own that exudes a sense of wonderment. Each sunrise sets the mood when planet earth gets ready to bathe in sparkling sunshine. Conversely, nightfall and sunsets bring a sense of relaxation and reflection.

In between sunrise and sunset, the air and landscapes and seascapes are overflowing with treasures we take for granted. Many of us go about our daily chores without noticing the beauty that surrounds us. Every tree, bush, plant or flower with its different shades adds to the wonderment of nature.

In an urban area, nature does get an assist by man, who plans and develops parks and recreational facilities. These developments resound to man's credit for his sense

Photo by: Diana Petersen

One of many beautiful things nature creates for us to enjoy.

of the aesthetics. Man's attempts to duplicate nature are laudable.

But to me, nature has no equal when it comes to raw and stark beauty. Specifically, I refer to one of my favorite retreats in California and the United States: the Trinity Alps. The surge of beauty and rugged serenity leaps up and engulfs one from all directions. One is both at peace and excited from the never-ending feast to the eye, as well as to the soul.

I feel blessed when I occasionally seek refuge in this sanctuary of striking beauty. In the city, man can view the landscape and proclaim his accomplishments from horizon to horizon.

But when I'm immersed in the natural world of a Yosemite or a Trinity Alps, I'm overwhelmed with appreciation and reverence with what nature and God have created.

Susan Kennedy

KGO Radio
Noon News Anchor

My favorite places in Northern California are Calistoga and Mendocino. I absolutely love the Mendocino coast. It's just a wonderful place to go when you really need to relax and get away from it all.

Calistoga is the ultimate rest and relaxation spot because of the hot pools, the mud baths, the massages and the wineries.

I like to stay in bed-and-breakfast inns or private cottages in Mendocino and in Calistoga. I like any of the wonderful spas.

One of Susan's restful hideaway's is the California coastline.

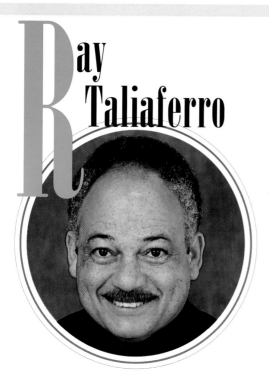

Ray Taliaferro

KGO Radio Talk Show Host

There are a number of beautiful places in Northern California; but I really like the Napa Wine Country. During the day, it's beautiful to take a trip to Lake Hennessey where you can see all kinds of beautiful birds, from egrets to herons. Once I saw a pair of bald eagles. I thought they just strayed in from elsewhere, because I don't think eagles live there year-round. It was just glorious seeing them flying around together.

I also enjoy going to the Joseph Phelps Winery, which is a place where you can picnic in a vineyard or on a hillside overlooking the vineyards. They'll even prepare it for you outdoors with a picnic table. You'll want to do that in the spring, because the winery has wisteria that are more than 90 years old. They cover trellises as large as a football field. The wisteria are absolutely beautiful.

For dinner, perhaps one of the most romantic restaurants I've ever been is The French Laundry in Yountville in the Napa Valley. Between courses you can get up from your table and walk out in the rose garden with the stars and the moon shining above, and then go back to your dinner and dessert. It's just a wonderful way to spend a weekend.

Do the lake and the winery during the day, and you can go

Bird watching at Lake Hennessey with Ray.

to The French Laundry at night. Then you are prepared to come back to San Francisco.

The meal is great, the hiking fantastic, and the homey environment make you want to come back for more.

My favorite place is the Beltane Ranch in Glen Ellen in the Sonoma Valley. It's a wonderful bed-and-breakfast inn with only four or five rooms.

When you turn down the driveway, you think you're in Ireland. The fences are rock, there's a big field, and the owner, Rosemary Wood, has her own garden. No matter what time of the year you go, it seems like she's growing herbs. I believe this estate was in her family long ago and was deserted. Rosemary returned and restored it. The setting is very comfortable. She has a tennis court, and there are fantastic hiking spots.

What I like about it is, not only the hospitality of the owner, but the beautiful setting in the Wine Country. You can ride your bike to various places from its location. It's reasonably priced, and the food is great.

You get a breakfast you've never had before: wonderful warm muffins just out of the oven, even popovers. Every time you go, there are strawberry or raspberry pancakes. And all this in an intimate, extremely homey setting.

Photo by: Verne Paule

The beautiful Beltane Ranch in Glen Ellen.

Chris Bjorklund

KGO Radio Consumer Reporter

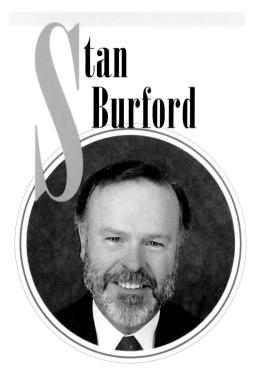

Stan Burford

KGO Radio
Traffic Anchor

A popular getaway for Stan and his wife is to drive an hour to where his daughter was married.

My favorite local trip is to drive up to Calistoga with my wife and do a little window shopping. Generally we end up coming home with an artifact from Calistoga, after having a wonderful lunch or dinner.

While in Calistoga, we usually visit Cloppick Goss Winery, which is right on Highway 29. This is the place where our daughter was married in 1994. (We like to go back and revisit the scene of the crime!)

We either have lunch or dinner, depending on the time of day, at a restaurant called Brava Terrace, which is on Highway 29. It's a great place with a very casual atmosphere and lovely food.

The whole thing is about an hour from where we live, which makes it very easy to visit at a drop of a hat. We have done this now probably six times in the last year and have never really grown tired of it because Calistoga and the surrounding area are always so different each time we visit. It's always a very exciting place to be.

Photo by: Verne Paule

Lincoln Avenue in downtown Calistoga.

Sit back and enjoy the ride, as Michaelynn takes you for a drive...

I've been thinking about my favorite place to go in the Bay Area. At first I couldn't think of one, but then the thought came to me. I decided one of my very favorite things to do is get on Highway 1 starting in Pacifica and drive south to Half Moon Bay. If time allows, I continue toward Santa Cruz, and if time really permits, I drive all the way to Monterey.

The best time to do this, and I've actually done it, is during a full moon. It is fantastic!

Whether you are with someone or by yourself, you can stop at numerous little places along the way. You can see them from the road, just tiny little places to visit or grab a cup of coffee. You are also only a short walk

The most glorious ride down the coast to Monterey.

from the water.

After you complete the trip, turn around and come back. The whole journey, from Pacifica to Santa Cruz and back, can be done in about three-and-a-half hours.

It's one of the most cleansing, refreshing, reflective, wonderful things you can do. You've got the ocean, the mountains, a stretch of time to think and it just makes you feel really good. Or you can cry and scream the whole time.

Michaelynn Meyers

KGO Radio Traffic Reporter

Tori Campbell

KGO Radio Traffic Anchor

You'll find Tori at _her_ favorite place.

When I first told my husband that I was going to write about our favorite beach in the Bay Area, he said, "Make sure you give the wrong directions."

I'm sure that is the reaction of many folks who are reluctant to give away the location of their secret getaways.

But our favorite place really is not a secret. It is the beaches along Pescadero on Highway 1, about 10 miles south of Half Moon Bay.

My husband used to go there when he went to high school in Woodside. When I moved to California, it was one of the first places he took me back in the summer of 1989.

Our most memorable visit there was Feb. 2, 1991.

We settled down for a nice picnic when he produced a little black box with a diamond ring inside and popped the question.

Now we go back every year around Valentine's Day for a picnic and a walk on the beach. This year we brought our young son, who loved it.

The sea air, the seagulls, the pounding surf opposite dramatic sandy cliffs makes it a world away from the San Ramon Valley, that's only a little more than a half-hour drive across the San Mateo Bridge.

Tori and her son Lawrence at the beach.

A favorite getaway for Gene Rusco is to take his wife and dogs to the beach - but not just any beach...

Let my wife, Linda, and me take you on a short, beautiful trip through diverse geography, breathtaking views and serene settings. Bring your dog.

We start on Big Basin Way in Saratoga where we'll get coffee-to-go, then up Highway 9 through the Santa Cruz Mountains. The highway takes you through the mountain towns of Boulder Creek, Ben Lomond and Felton. Reaching Santa Cruz, we head south on Highway 1. We're going to the beach, but not the crowded beaches seen by most out-of-towners.

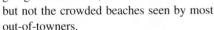
Sir Rasquel at Carmel Beach.

We exit Highway 1 at Rio Del Mar south of Capitola, then turn right at the end of the exit. Traveling about a block, we will turn left into Clubhouse Drive, and continue through the golf course (noticing the beautiful homes and the landscaping) to Sumner Avenue. Turning left, we head toward the Seascape Resort, where we park on the street. Walking through the resort, we follow the cement pathway to the beach. From there you can see south to Moss Landing and north to Santa Cruz. It's a huge beach with very few people. We could spend the afternoon, but we're going south.

There are few places in the country more animal-friendly than Carmel-by-the-Sea. There are no leash laws on the beaches, just reminders that responsible people clean up after their animals. We stay (with our dogs) at Doris Day's Cypress Inn. The Inn has a book with menus from area restaurants. We like to visit a deli and pack a small picnic to the beach.

When you go, watch for a smiling couple with a Lhasa and Shi Tzu.

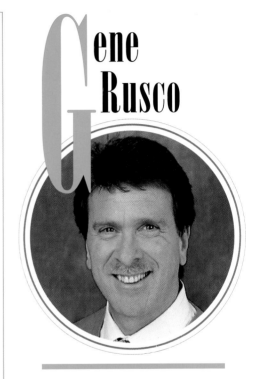

Gene Rusco

KGO Radio
South Bay Bureau Chief

Michael Luckoff

KGO Radio
President and General Manager

Transfer me anywhere as long as it's half-way between Carmel and Lake Tahoe.

The problem with determining my favorite place or thing to do in Northern California is that it's hard to limit it to a few choices. I enjoy golf, tennis, running, hiking and boating. If anything, it's frustrating because there are so many things to do and so little time to do them.

Bay Area cuisine is the greatest. From Terra in St. Helena, to Postrio in San Francisco, to Fresh Cream in Monterey, there is fabulous eating. The only concerns that can hold you back are the fit of your clothes and your waistline.

I love the Napa Valley. Marin County is a great place to live, and San Francisco is an incredible place to earn one's livelihood. Then there's Lake Tahoe and the Monterey Peninsula – what more can I say?

As I've told my employers, they can transfer me anywhere they want as long as it's half-way between Carmel and Lake Tahoe.

Photo by: Verne Paule

The beauty and splendor of the Monterey area.

Bernie Ward

KGO Radio
Talk Show Host

My favorite place to go and thing to do in Northern California is to sleep in my bed at home.

I host a talk show every day of the week: my weeknight newstalk show, my national talk show and my Sunday "Godtalk" show. That's a lot of hours on KGO Radio, so you can understand why I'd like to get a little sleep!

Shann Nix

KGO Radio
Talk Show Host

One of my very favorite things to do in the Bay Area is to go to a book store in Mill Valley. I'll buy a new book, a cup of coffee and a muffin and sit in the sun and read and drink until I'm sunburned. Then I'll go over to Jimmy Lowe's and have the most wonderful crab puffs, and then to the Sweetwater to hear a really good down-and-dirty blues band. My perfect afternoon, all in Mill Valley!

Ken Hunt

KGO Radio
Reporter

The best place to go in Northern California is any winery in the Napa or Sonoma Valleys - as long as they are open for tasting.

Frogs Leap is a very nice winery which makes a great red wine and has really cool corks that say "rib-bit" on them.

Then there's Chateau Mount Helena, which has a Japanese garden that offers a picnic. You don't think of a Japanese garden in the wine country, but it's wonderful.

Bryna Laub

KGO Radio Talk Show Host

A favorite romantic weekend for Bryna is a place just like the place where she grew up.

I love Monterey. I grew up in New England; and the Monterey area, which was actually settled as a whaling village, reminds me so much of New England. It's like going home. The climate is perfect for strolling on the beach in your shorts and t-shirt. It's not like you're in a bathing suit competition, which is what it's like at Southern California beaches.

There's also great golf. And I don't have to mention that there's incredible food everywhere. If you're there to celebrity-watch, you won't be disappointed. There are tons of them hanging out from Monterey to Carmel.

Monterey is also the only place where you can find many hotels and inns with working fireplaces and extras like feather beds. So if you want a romantic weekend away, the finest spot has to be the Monterey area.

Photo by: Verne Pate

Bryna enjoys the Monterey coast.

It sounds like a cliche, but I think the wine country in Northern California is the best. It reminds me of the saying, "The prophet not honored in his own land." A lot of people who were born here or have lived here a long time forget about the great resources in the wine-country regions of Napa, Sonoma and Mendocino Counties. Of course, you can go south to the wine country, too. But I prefer the Northern California wine country.

It's very affordable for a weekend stay. There are small bed-and-breakfast inns with wonderful breakfasts and beautiful accommodations available for a reasonable price. There are also very expensive places where they have spas and other luxuries.

Almost all of the wineries offer tours, and most still offer tastings at no charge.

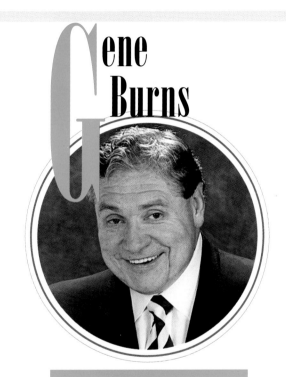

Gene Burns

KGO Radio
Talk Show Host

The restaurants are some of the finest in the world. There's Terra and Tra Vigne in St. Helena, Wappo in Calistoga, Mustard's Grill, Stars Grill, and there are little sandwich shops and out-of-the-way places where you can buy wonderful breads.

And you can pack a picnic lunch and go to a vineyard like the Shramsberg Champagne Cellars. You can't even see it from Highway 29, but when you head up the road it's like you've entered a state park. It's really remarkable, and it has picnic facilities. (Food isn't sold on the property, so bring your own.).

So I would say: remember the Wine Country, even if you've lived here all of your life. Take in the wineries and enjoy the wonderful restaurants. It's only an hour away from San Francisco, and it's a great place for a getaway weekend.

RJ Peruman

KGO Radio Reporter

My favorite place to take my family is the redwoods way up in Northern California. We just head north on Highway 101 into Humboldt County, and if we have time we keep going to the state park in Del Norte County near the state line.

In Humboldt County, I really enjoy the Avenue of the Giants. There are a lot of great campgrounds and fun activities for the kids. The whole area is just absolutely beautiful. And staying in a campground is an inexpensive way to go. There are plenty of nearby stores, so it's not really "roughing it."

There are lots of day trips available from the central campground areas, everything within an hour or less.

There's great hiking and great fishing. We like to go rafting on the Eel River.

If we want to stay a little closer to the Bay Area, or just take a day trip, I think the Marin Headlands and Mount Tamalpais are absolute jewels. Sometimes Muir Woods can be crowded, but there's so much else to see in the area. Muir Beach is great, as is the whole Headlands area. On a clear day, I don't think you can beat it.

Photo by: Verne Paule

The great redwoods in Humboldt County.

My favorite trip has great food, a nice room and it's near the water.

My favorite trip is driving down to Big Sur and staying at the beaches. I like to stay at Deetjens Big Sur Inn right on the Pacific Coast Highway.

Leaving San Francisco and driving down the Pacific Coast Highway, which is one of the most beautiful drives in the world, you can just feel all the stress and worries falling away from you. And when you finally reach Big Sur, suddenly you're under this canopy of redwoods. You're deep in the woods, but right on the ocean at the same time. The smell is just terrific. Soon you reach Deetjens Big Sur Inn.

The inn looks like a little cabin. In fact, it smells the way our 150-year-old cabin in

A lovely stroll overlooking Big Sur.

Photo by: Diana Petersen

northern Michigan smells. Each room has its own character. My favorite place to stay is the Antique Apartment which has two different beds and is real rustic looking. There are always fresh flowers on the table, and the pot-belly stove is all set up for a fire. Nearby, there are all these little cabins tucked in a redwood forest, with the ocean right in front of you. The price is really great. But you should call for reservations.

The food is wonderful, and the service is great. The menu offers terrific fish dinners, and the wine list is first-rate. And don't miss the Sunday breakfast: fresh blueberry pancakes and great coffee. Everything's made from the produce grown in the area.

After a weekend in Big Sur, I'm prepared to return to the stresses of the city.

Mary Ellen Geist

KGO Radio Reporter

Joanie Greggains

KGO Radio
Talk Show Host

The great outdoors is where you'll find Joanie.

My favorite thing to do is hike in the Russian River area which offers a wide variety of trails.

If you want to hike in the woods, there's Armstrong Woods, which has easy trails for the less physically fit and tougher trails in the hills for the more active hiker.

I also like the Pomo Canyon hike. It starts at Goat Rock Beach and goes for six miles into Pomo Canyon. This is actually where Pomo Indians lived.

Another great walk in the same area is from Goat Rock to the town of Jenner, where you can duck into the River Inn and have a cup of coffee before you head back.

The best part about the Russian River area is that it's unspoiled. It offers such a great variety of places to hike, and it's really very beautiful.

I like to hike with friends, my dog and my fabulous cat, Betty, who likes to ride in my backpack.

Another way to enjoy the Russian River area is to canoe or kayak all the away from Guerneville to Monte Rio. And if you're really brave and have an ocean-going kayak, you can keep going to Jenner and the mouth of the river. It's a great way to get outdoors.

There's plenty to do along the Russian River, and it's only an hour north of San Francisco.

Joanie and Betty enjoy a nice hike at Goat Rock.

Whenever possible, you'll find Jon outdoors.

I really enjoy the great outdoors.

One of my favorite places to go (but I don't get there nearly as often as I'd like) is Yosemite National Park. I'm not a mountain climber, but I dearly love the breathtaking beauty that Yosemite offers. I go there maybe once every few years.

I love Glacier Point. It affords the whole view of the valley. I enjoy the beautiful Mariposa Grove, and the Wawona campground, where I stayed the last time I was there. Also don't miss Yosemite Falls.

Vernal Falls Trail is another favorite of mine. In fact, the last time I was there I hiked all the way up to Nevada Falls, where you get a view right down on the water-

Jon Bristow

KGO Radio
Noon News Anchor and Reporter

fall. It's magnificent.

What can I say? Yosemite is a unique place. There is no spot like it in the world, and it's right here in Northern California. It's a gem.

Another favorite place is in the redwood country of Humboldt County. There's the Avenue of the Giants and Humboldt Redwoods State Park — both fabulous places. You can get lost in those huge trees where day can suddenly turn into night. It's awesome to have those ancient trees towering over you.

I also like to go to the zoo in any city I'm in. I love wild animals, particularly the big cats. It's one way to explore the world of wildlife in an urban setting.

Pete Wilson

Governor of California

My favorite places to visit allow me to indulge my three favorite pastimes — reading, hiking, and enjoying breathtaking scenery. Of all the beautiful places in Northern California, Yosemite is particularly special for me.

With its majestic granite formations, spectacular waterfalls, pristine meadows, and tranquil Merced River, Yosemite is the perfect setting to relax and unwind. I enjoy walking in the meadows at dusk, watching the Mule deer graze, and breathing crisp, clean air that hasn't been filtered through an office.

I also enjoy morning hikes to Yosemite Falls and Half Dome. And after a long day of tramping around the park, it's a great pleasure to settle down in the Ahwahnee Hotel with a good book.

Yosemite holds many special memories for me, and I can't wait to return.

Photo by: Verne Paule

The majestic beauty of a sunset at Yosemite.

John Poimiroo

Deputy Secretary Director of Tourism

Dozens of images come to mind when people think of California, but for me, the redwood forests are the most special.

Whether they be powerful groves of massive Giant Sequoias (Sequoiadendron Giganteum) that are rooted in the high Sierra, or the more lofty Coastal Redwoods (Sequoiadendron Sempervirens) of the North Coast, redwood groves are spiritual places wholly Californian.

My favorite groves are in the northwest corner of California at Redwood National Park and Redwood State Park. Jedediah Smith Redwoods State Park, northernmost of the redwood stands in Del Norte County, is a rain forest inhabited by the big trees and carpeted with emerald ferns and pink azalea sprouting from a forest floor littered with fallen giants.

Only the most hardened can stand in a redwood forest and not sense the Almighty. As sunlight points to earth in shafts of silver, one immediately understands why they are called cathedral groves.

Photo by: Verne Paule

There is nothing that can match the strength and overwhelming beauty of the redwoods.

Lynn Ferrin

**Editor & Manager
Motorland Magazine**

It is the single most recognizable mountain in the Sierra – arguably in the whole country. As an East Coast schoolgirl I knew its name years before I beheld its perfectly rounded bald pate, its neatly sliced-off face turned down the Valley of Yosemite, as if it were searching for its other half.

If you are a true rambler of the Range of Light, you must certainly in your career climb Half Dome. In midsummer thousands of hikers do it, yet it isn't particularly easy.

You'll find the trailhead at Happy Isles, a shuttlebus stop at the east end of Yosemite Valley. From there to the Dome's highest point, it's a steady grind of eight miles, up almost 5,000 feet – one way. The trail is paved as far as Vernal Falls, then horse-dusty to the top of Nevada Falls. Well back from the waterfall, the pools of the Merced River beckon a refreshing dip in late summer. From there, it's a steady climb up through the forest of

A perfect day to climb Half Dome.

Photo by: Lynn Ferrin

pine and fir. The last water source before the summit is the little off-trail spring before the scary switchbacks, known to some as the Granite Staircase.

The last bit of the trail is the most daunting: a 900-foot ladder of steel cables and wooden crossbars, strung up against the slick granite shoulder. And there's the terror of afternoon lightning, which has stolen from too many hikers the opportunity of coming down alive.

But still, the 8,842-foot summit of Half Dome is a fine and commanding place to be, smooth and silver, surprisingly vast. The view is heady — down Yosemite Valley to El Capitan and the tumbled foothills, up Tenaya Canyon to Cathedral Peak, southeast to the Clark Range. If you've a stomach of steel, you can crawl to the edge and peer down that awful dark face, sheared by the journeywork of ice — and sometimes see real climbers crawling up the hard way, with ropes and harnesses.

These days most people are compelled to go up and down in one day. Camping is no longer allowed on the summit (to protect the oblivious but endangered Mount Lyell salamander, which dwells among the rocks there). Most of the camping en route for backpackers is at Little Yosemite Valley, but wilderness permits are hard to come by as it lies along the John Muir Trail, the most popular backcountry route in Yosemite National Park. In any case, you'd spend most of the night screeching at the black bears.

So, you'll need to start by dawn, and carry a daypack well-stacked with water, food and rain gear. When it's over, and you've staggered back down to Happy Isles, you will have walked 16 miles and gone up and down almost 10,000 feet. Your legs will be trembling jelly. You will have seen the elephant.

The cables are usually in place on Half Dome from late May to early October.

Allison Hodges

KGO Radio's Media & Community Relations Manager

Close to home (I live in San Francisco), I enjoy hiking in the Marin Headlands. There's a five-mile trail that loops around; it's a pretty tough uphill climb, but you get a great workout. From the top you can see the Golden Gate Bridge and San Francisco, and on the other side you have a spectacular view of Marin.

A little farther from home I love Sonoma. Whether it's wine-tasting, picnicking, trying out one of the many fabulous restaurants, staying at the Sonoma Mission Inn (great pool and wonderful massages!), or just enjoying the sunshine and fresh air, Sonoma is always a favorite destination.

And for a little more activity (but not too much), I recommend canoeing on the Russian River. On a warm summer day, pack drinks and a lunch in an ice chest, put on your bathing suit, and enjoy the beautiful river. There are

KGO Radio crew at the Sonoma Mission Inn: (l-r) Reporter Mary Ellen Geist, ABC News Correspondent Greg Jarrett, Christopher Thompson, Marketing Director Darcy Provo, Engineer Paul Zorich and Allison Hodges.

some areas with faster moving water, but for the most part it's an easy paddle downstream. The outfit that rents canoes has a shuttle bus that will pick you up at the end and bring you back to your car.

Karen Reid

KGO Radio Engineer

In my opinion, a vacation is not really a vacation without working up a good sweat. Thus my propensity for bicycle touring. Touring by bicycle allows one to *experience* an area, rather than simply *see* it.

A fully–supported ride around the lake will help you appreciate Lake Tahoe from a fresh, new perspective. Pick up *California Bicyclist,* a free magazine, at your favorite bike shop for the specifics of the 72-mile ride, which starts at Zephyr Cove in early June.

Riding in a group is always preferable on the narrow road encircling Lake Tahoe. In addition to the safety factor, the biggest advantage of an organized ride is the abundance of fruit, power drinks and peanut butter sandwiches.

If you must ride alone, stock up on water, power bars, spare tires and a patch kit. Ride mid-week in either early or late summer.

Be aware that the Tahoe Ride was once re-named "America's Most Blizzardly Bike Ride," for obvious reasons. Share the experience with a friend, or, better yet, your dad.

Karen and her dad in Lake Tahoe.

Adrienne Jennings
Big Brothers/Big Sisters of Marin

There are many places of varied sorts around the Bay Area that I have enjoyed, and just about anybody of any age can visit for little or no cost. Trips to the Marine Mammal Center, hiking the Marin coastal trails and going to local parades are just a few examples.

My Big Sister, Mary (I got matched with her four years ago -- one of the best experiences I've ever had), and I have found it fun to stroll the Farmers Market in San Rafael, sampling the scrumptious fares, and then do something like buzz out to the Pet-a-Llama Ranch (in Petaluma) and observe the animals. Another of my favorite outings was camping with Mary at Big Sur. That included going to beaches and on waterfall hikes.

Going to Guide Dogs for the Blind to see one of the monthly graduations of newly trained dogs is free and about as wonderful an experience as you can imagine. Call 415-499-4000 for the next graduation date and time.

We are fortunate to live in an area with so many diverse places to experience.

Kevin Fuller

Big Brothers/Big Sisters of Marin

Our Yosemite trip was fun. It was the best trip we ever had. The drive up was fun, but long. We saw cows and a large smelly bull in a field by the road. We stopped to take a picture of him, but he ran away. We also stopped at the Hershey factory, but we missed taking the tour and we wanted to get to the lodge before dark. That night we went to a musical in town, where we heard the local townspeople sing songs from Broadway shows.

The following day on our way into Yosemite Park we got to see three different kinds of weather: cloudy, snowy and sunny. We stopped at Bridal Veil waterfall and got all wet and cold, but had a great time. After lunch we went to Yosemite Falls and hiked a little on the trail and climbed rocks. On our way back, we stopped to look at some deer in the meadow, and we smelled a skunk.

Kevin & his Big Brother Shel at Yosemite

Anita Jones

1995 Regional Big Sister of the Year Big Brothers/Big Sisters of Marin

The spectacular views of the Pacific Ocean and Golden Gate Bridge are rewards enough for making the trip to Baker Beach in San Francisco's Presidio area. This historic sandy stretch is also an invigorating spot for a beach-blanket breakfast.

If you relish the feel of an ocean breeze on your face and the sound of waves rushing in, try this simple recipe:

1. Pack your favorite pastries and hot beverage.
2. Bundle up and bring sand chairs and blankets.
3. Find a good spot on the beach and settle in.
4. Enjoy the views.
5. If you like to fish, bring a pole and cast.

Make this trip often and you can decide which time of day and which time of year you favor the most.

Photo by: Ron Roehrick

Big Sister Anita Jones (left) and her Little Sister, Aleite Roberts share a moment of fun on Baker Beach.

Coming Up Next...

Photo by: Diana Petersen

Beach

HELPFUL TIPS

Bed & Breakfast/Inns

highlights

THINGS TO DO

Beach

PISMO BEACH

One of my favorite California spots is Shell Beach. The sunsets are so radiantly beautiful. My husband, Jay, of 34 years and I love it there. Some days we go into Pismo Beach for awhile and race back to Shell Beach to catch the sunset from our motel deck. It's an artist's dream.

At Pismo Beach a few years ago, I did the "California" drive on the beach. I managed to get our brand new truck stuck deep enough in the sand to have to have it pulled out. Just another weekend in California.

There's so much to see and do in our great state.

Submitted by Marla Kreidler

TILLWATER COVE

It was the day after Christmas 1989, and I announced to my family that we were going on a "field trip" to our favorite beach.

Even before we left our home in the Almaden Valley of San Jose, our youngest daughter, Cathleen, asked, "Can we got some cinnamon rolls and hot chocolate in Carmel?" "Of course," was our reply. Tina, my wife, and Marisa, our oldest daughter, wanted to make sure we were going to schedule time to visit the quaint boutique shops at the Pebble Beach Lodge.

We left at 8 a.m. and arrived at Ocean Avenue in Carmel by 9:30 a.m. After breakfast, we entered the breathtaking 17 Mile Drive and motored to the Lodge at Pebble Beach. As soon as we arrived, we made luncheon reservations at the dining room. Our window table provided 180-degree views of the rocky coastline. Everyone enjoyed a truly gourmet lunch of cream of artichoke soup and fresh lake trout. Following lunch, we strolled southward along the world famous 18th fairway down to "our" favorite beach, Stillwater Cove. It was so warm: short-sleeved shirts were just about perfect.

The weather, scenery and nature's wildlife brought a special happiness and joy that our family has long treasured.

Submitted by Tim Pacelli

DILLON BEACH

If you are a double-whammy beach lover and clam digger, Dillon Beach in Marin County is the place to go. You'll be dazzled by the rural scenery all along the way; and, once you arrive, you can pick and choose from swimming, surfing, boogie-boarding, jet skiing, windsurfing, skim-boarding, surf or pokepole fishing, tide-pooling and my all-time favorite, digging for horseneck clams. It is truly a muddy adventure resulting in such culinary rewards as clam fritters, clam

CiCi Zerbe enjoys the scenery at Shelter Cove.

GETAWAYS

linguine and clam chowder. The clam barge runs during the summer months, or you can dig away along the shore at low tide.

Dillon Beach, near Tomales Bay, is located 65 miles north of San Francisco and 120 miles from Sacramento. Many parts of America are known for beautiful coasts; but I've concluded that nothing can match the unsurpassed beauty of the California coast and its jewel, Dillon Beach.

Submitted by Maureen B. Cassidy

SHELTER COVE

What has not changed since the '50s at Shelter Cove is the four and a half miles of accessible tidal beach front, which is of great interest to scientists and tourists alike. Offshore rocks, kelp beds and tidal areas are inhabited by seals, sea lions, a variety of marine birds and a multitude of sea life. There are anemones big

enough to put your fist in. Yet almost any day of the year you can be the first to put your foot prints on the sand.

Another pastime in Shelter Cove is whale watching. Add to this the Black Sand Beach, which extends to the mouth of the Mattole River. Shelter Cove's protected harbor provides swimming for the young and year-round beachcombing. Winter storms bring in driftwood and many other treasures for collectors. Hiking trails wind around the mountains, including one to King's Peak, with an elevation of 4,086 feet. This is the highest point on the continental U.S. shoreline. Fishermen are attracted to the Cove because of its outstanding deep-sea salmon fishing. Ling/rock cod, red/black snapper, abalone, crab and shellfish are also abundant in local waters.

Access to Shelter Cove is provided by an all-weather, paved county road from the Garberville/Redway exit off Highway 101.

Submitted by CiCi & John Zerbe

MANCHESTER BEACH

One of my favorite places anywhere is the northern coast of California. I especially love Manchester State Beach. It is seven miles north of Point Arena on Highway 1.

There are sand dunes and all kinds of driftwood to explore. It's a great place to walk or just sit and relax. While at Manchester Beach, you can visit other small beaches in the area.

Submitted by Star Norris

Top: Clam digging at Dillon Beach.
2nd from top: A great view of Pismo Beach.
Bottom right; Christmas time at Stillwater Cove.
Bottom left: Relaxing day at Manchester State Beach.

More Beach

SEACLIFF BEACH

We are blessed with living near Sea Cliff Beach, where we walk every day.

The ocean is like a performing musical on stage. Every day it changes its act. It's so beautiful.

Photo by: Verne Paule

The good look at Seacliff Beach.

The concrete ship, The Palo Alto, is awesome to watch, as the ocean tries so hard to combat her.

Submitted by John E. Graham

SANTA CRUZ BEACH

I would like to tell you about a special place my entire family has gone to for more than 40 years. It is the Terrace Court Motel in Santa Cruz. The Terrace Court is located at 125 Beach St. across the street from the beach, wharf and boardwalk. It is a family-oriented motel and it's especially well-kept. Most of the little apartments have kitchenettes and are equipped with stove, refrigerator, toaster, coffee pots, basic dishes, pots and pans and utensils. All linens are provided.

We have often rented several rooms, having family reunions there and a few Thanksgiving and Christmas holidays, too. And there's maid service the next day to clean up. What a deal.

Submitted by Dave Cunningham

MacKERRICHER STATE BEACH

A beachcomber's delight is waiting to be discovered within MacKerricher State Park, located three miles north of Fort Bragg on Highway 1. There are miles of beaches to be explored, each with a distinctively different personality. There are rocky bluffs with crashing breakers, and rolling dunes with some of the softest sand anywhere to bury your feet in. The most intriguing aspect of this park for our family is the rich tide pool area, where we can literally spend hours carefully treading the rocks to discover sea stars, shore and hermit crabs, purple urchins, and giant green anemone in their inter-tidal homes. What a treat to quietly observe these fragile creatures, and what a valuable lesson on the balance of nature.

Another great feature of this park is the population of harbor seals, who sun themselves within easy view on the rocky bluffs of Laguna Point. There is a raised wooden walkway out to the seal viewing area, which makes this treat accessible to handicapped visitors. An eight-mile-long former logging road stretches the entire length of the park, offering spectacular ocean views to walkers and bicyclists alike. While the

The Aquirre family at MacKerricher Beach.

entire Fort Bragg-Mendocino area boasts a wealth of recreational opportunities, it is the special lure of MacKerricher State Park that brings our family back to the North Coast each year.

Submitted by Jean Aquirre

APTOS BEACH

For me, it's all in our village of Aptos and surrounding areas. My favorite companion is my 10-year-old granddaughter, Sarah. Aptos is five miles south of Santa Cruz on Highway 1.

Our fun day starts with an early morning fishing trip to the old Cement Ship at Seacliff Beach State Park. We fish for perch, smelt, or whatever chooses to bite on our hooks. After several hours, our catch on a good day may be four or five perch and one or two kingfish. We clean our fish at the designated area on the wharf.

After putting the fish in my refrigerator, we clean ourselves up and choose one of our two favorite spots for lunch. If we are feeling elegant, we head for the Veranda Room at the 125-year-old Bayview Hotel, an historic treasure, or a Chinese lunch at Uncle Kwok's Szechwan Restaurant.

Then it's off to the Santa Cruz Beach Boardwalk to play Fascination, a bingo-like ball game that has been there since I was a child. Finally, our day ends when we go home and prepare our Seacliff Supper, which has been the same for more than 50 years in our family. It consists of our catch-of-the-

Margaret and Sarah at the Bayview Hotel.

day, pan fried, and boiled potatoes smashed with a fork and buttered, and sliced tomatoes sprinkled with sugar.

Bon appetite. Come down to the beach.

Submitted by Margaret Vaughan

PINNACLE BEACH

One of our favorite things to do in California is to take the Pinnacle Gulch Trail, located in Bodega Harbor right off Highway 1 at Bodega Bay.

To get to Pinnacle Gulch you take South Harbor Drive off the coastal highway and follow the signs to a small parking area across the street from the trail.

You come out onto a very secluded beach hemmed in by cliffs and huge rocks. If you are lucky enough to be there at low tide, you can walk to Doran Beach. Unlike Doran Beach, its neighbor, Pinnacle Beach, still has a very rugged and primitive environment.

It's been said that Bodega Bay is east of Scotland and north of Pebble Beach. If you hike the Pinnacle Gulch Trail to the beach, you will feel you are just this side of heaven.

Submitted by the Cohn Family

BEACH AT SAN QUENTIN

My favorite spot is the little quiet beach on the road to San Quentin Prison. I'm not sure it has a name, so I'll just refer to it as the Beach at San Quentin. To get there take the Highway 580 exit in San Rafael. Turn off at the last exit before the Richmond Bridge. Go right and stop under the first trees by the water.

I usually run down there on a moment's notice. It always seems to be a peaceful place for me. Nice little sandy beach. Some rocks and fishing. Very quiet.

Submitted by Susan Bruce

The Cohn family at Doran Beach.

HELPFUL TIPS WHILE TRAVELING

Submitted by Jim Bodrero, Gray Line of San Francisco
38 years motor-coach driver (Retired)

After 38 years driving a motor coach, my concern about traveling is that you get there safely.

To begin with, have your vehicle checked and tuned including tires, brakes and all fluids topped off. You should also take along some extra coolant, auto transmission fluid, power-steering fluid, and oil and windshield washer fluid.

Next, do a "walk-a -round." Check all lights, turn signals, backup lights, four-way flashers and brake lights.

You should also carry tire chains, even though you may not be going into snow country. They are useful to have along for getting unstuck in other conditions.

You're On Your Way

Try to start early when you are rested and fresh and plan your drive in one hour periods, especially if you have youngsters. When you gas up, let children walk around a bit which gives them some exercise. If you've stopped in an interesting little town,

take some time to explore it. At each stop, trade off walking the youngsters with your traveling companion.

Notes on adverse weather...

In my experience, the most dangerous and tiresome driving is in heavy fog. It requires constant concentration which becomes very tedious. Almost all fog accidents are caused by fatigue and inattention, especially at night. If you must drive in heavy fog, take breaks more frequently than you would driving in normal conditions. Always drive with your headlights on low beam—this will cut the glare. Put your lights on low beam during the daytime. Some of the worst fog conditions are found in California's Central Valley in the winter, especially around the heavily traveled holiday season.

In normal driving conditions you should use the four-second rule. When the car ahead of you passes a fixed object (bridge, overpass, shadow, etc.), it should be four seconds before you pass the same object. This formula holds true at almost any speed. It allows you enough time to react to the car in front of you if it stops suddenly. The four-second rule should be extended in adverse weather conditions such as fog, snow, rain or icy conditions.

Black Ice

First of all, black ice looks like dry pavement. It is caused when snow or slush is slightly warmed during the day only to freeze again at night. Black ice also occurs during the day in places on the road that remain in the shade all day.

If you encounter black ice and you feel your car start to drift, treat your brakes and gas pedals as if you have eggs under your foot. Keep your wheels turning; this will help give your car direction. Steer gently. Don't lock your brakes!!! Brakes don't stop your car...they stop the wheels. The tires provide no traction or direction if they are not turning.

Snow

When it is time to chain-up, here are some tips. When you use cable chains, SET THE PARKING BRAKE. Installation is fairly easy working only with straps and buckles. Cable chains are fairly good on ice, but not very effective in deep snow.

When you use link chains, SET THE PARKING BRAKE. Lay chains in front of your front tire, cross-link hooks away from the tire and chain clips facing the rear. Roll your car forward so that both ends are clear. Loosely fasten outside clip and hook, then fasten inside clip and hook firmly. Now fasten outside clip and hook firmly. After you install both chains, roll the car ahead a short distance to loosen the chains. Take up slack, if needed; then install your rubber slack adjusters, if provided or if necessary.

Many people prefer to use spring installers or jack up the car. Use whichever method you prefer.

Also, I recommend using dishwashing gloves over light wool gloves to install chains—they really work.

Many people prefer to use spring installers or jack up the car. Use whichever method you prefer.

While driving in snow, remember that traction is the key. Apply brakes and power gently. Don't spin or lock your wheels. I know of many "four wheelers" who have 300 horsepower and think that they can get anywhere, but just ask any snow country tow truck driver what really happens.

After leaving the snow area, try not to drive too much on dry pavement with chains. They get really hot and it ruins the metal links.

I hope these notes will help our "On the Go'ers" to enjoy being "On the Go."

Bed & Breakfast Inns

Country Rose Bed and Breakfast Inn

There is a place in my community that others might find interesting. I live in the Gilroy-San Martin area, and our big annual event is the Garlic Festival. However, I don't want to talk about that. I want to tell everyone about a bed and breakfast inn that I occasionally stay at, or use, or just visit.

The name is Country Rose Inn Bed and Breakfast. The thing that makes it so appealing is the elegance of the decor and the personal touch the innkeeper, Rose Hernandez, gives. She has decorated the place with antiques, some reflecting her heritage.

It's a must, even if you're not going to the Garlic Festival.

Submitted by Thelma Ledbetter

The Gate House Inn

One of our favorite weekends is at a wonderful turn-of-the-century Victorian, The Gate House, located in the town of Jackson. The setting is lovely, especially in the springtime.

The hillsides are surrounded by a bucolic countryside. It is peaceful, romantic, and there are many things to do, such as play golf, water sports, or stroll.

The Gate House is just a short walk from the famous Teresa's restaurant, and barely a mile to the center of Jackson, where you can shop in the many lovely shops. If you're interested in antiques, you'll enjoy the many antique shops in Jackson and surrounding small towns.

We would highly recommend this lovely Victorian bed and breakfast. The service and hospitality are excellent. There are many things to say about a weekend in this area, but one would have to experience it for himself or herself to appreciate the beauty and excitement it has to offer.

Submitted by George & Joyce Medeiros

W hat a great find! Friends told us of a very special place, and we are really glad they did.

The world-class Bell Glen Resort is on the banks of the scenic Eel River. It actually has four distinct aspects. There are six elegant, private, spotless B & B cabins (the housekeeper is Swiss-trained), each beautifully decorated with

Bell Glen Resort

antiques, curios, teddy bears and private redwood decks overlooking the river. There's complimentary wine, coffee, tea, and hot chocolate with marshmallows in each cabin, and breakfast is brought right to your door. Various cabins have honeymoon tubs-for-two, a fireplace or a jacuzzi. There's also a sauna and jacuzzi on the grounds. Wonderful dinners are available in the dining room or in the international bistro/pub, hosted by a great bartender who loves sharing local lore and redwood factoids.

The resort also has a European-style youth hostel for adventuresome travelers from all over the world. There's a large kitchen, private and semi-private cottages and a teepee.

Congenial innkeepers Gene and Sandy Barnett go out of their way to give you a great stay, in either the B & B or the youth hostel. It's a great change from the city. We highly recommend it.

Submitted by Sherry Marincich

S ampling various bed and breakfast inns around the Gold Country is great fun. There are numerous quaint restaurants and cafes in each Gold Country town. And I

Gold Quartz Bed & Breakfast Inn

can report that the past is still present in this part of the state.

Ever so special to us is the Gold Quartz Inn in the area of picturesque Sutter Creek. It's a large new Queen Anne building constructed to resemble Victorian grandeur. The elegant, individually decorated rooms are exceptionally large and each one has a television and VCR. We've never been in a more comfortable room in a more comfortable place. It was romantic and cozy in every way.

The delightful afternoon buffet tea included numerous homemade appetizers, pastries, cakes and local wines. This was a meal in itself. The morning is definitely started on the right track with a generous full breakfast buffet served in the dining room. The friendly and knowledgeable staff is happy to accommodate your every need.

The Gold Quartz Inn is charming, incorporating the style of the past with all the conveniences of the present.

Submitted by Sherry Busalacchi

highlights

1. One of my favorite places to go is San Pablo Dam. It has a big lake and lots of trees. It is very pretty. We like to go fishing there with my family. We go there really early in the morning and bring lots of food and drinks and spend the whole day. There are lots of picnic tables and barbecue pits. You can fish off the docks, and sometimes you catch lots of fish.

There is a little store where you can buy fishing bait. There are also a lot of frogs and tadpoles in the water that are fun to catch. My papa has a boat that we bring sometimes, and we take turns going out fishing. That's a lot of fun!

It's fun to put your feet off the dock and into the water. The water is very cold. It's a great place - you should go.

Submitted by Nicole Miller - Age 7

1. Nicole, along with her friends, taking time out from fishing to pose for the camera. 2. Enjoying the weekends as a Civil War family. 3. Happy 80th birthday with (l-r): Joan, Evelyn, Don and Ardyth. 4. Danielle, age 5, enjoying a pumpkin at the Fesitval.

2. One of my favorite weekend trips is to join my daughter and her husband at a Civil War re-enactment.

When my son-in-law climbs into his gray, itchy, woolen uniform, cotton shirt, straps on his Sam Browne belt, sets his kepie (cap) on his head, hoists his black-powder, single-shot rifle onto his shoulder, I know we're in for another walk back into the pages of history. My daughter puts on her three petticoats, her long cotton dress, covers her long hair with a snood (hair net), picks up her drawstring purse, and walks from the cotton-tented encampment to the battlefield.

Yes, they have a real battle with horses, swords, cannon, loud black powder, and several units of foot soldiers. Both sides are represented. There is always lots of noise, clouds of smoke, confusion, men falling down with bloody wounds, and women rushing to assist the wounded.

After the battle you are given a lecture about the Civil War, and everyone who participates talks about their character.

There is also a group selling memorabilia from the Civil War era. You can purchase costumes, uniforms and antiques.

Submitted by Nancy Larson

3. My three children took me on a rainy day to Fort Bragg. The redwoods in the grove along the Navarro River were still beautiful. My favorite motel in Fort Bragg overlooks the beach, and you can see an occasional boat going out to sea.

Our fish dinner in Noyo Harbor was enhanced by the view of fishing boats returning to harbor.

There was a Farmers Market that day. Sweet, juicy strawberries and floral bouquets found their way back to our motel.

Our next stop was at the Mendocino Coast Botanical Gardens. We took a walk through the beautiful gardens to view the thousands of native plants, and to purchase a few.

Next we went down the coast to Saint Ores in Gualala. We were welcomed at the weathered, onion-domed structure, given a cocktail of our choice, and into the woods we went to our cottage. From our little deck was a clear view of the ocean and, to my delight, deer feeding in an old apple orchard. In the evening, pate, champagne, and back to dine. Choices of wild game and fish served in a unique manner.

Breakfast was served on the sunlit deck viewing the ocean, and we had the treat of seeing wild turkeys feeding in the orchard.

The next day we went to Bodega Bay for lunch at the Inn at the Tides.

Memories were renewed and new ones added. The deepening pleasure was being in the company of my two daughters and son.

Submitted by Evelyn M. Bush, 80 years young

4. Our family's favorite thing to do in the Bay Area is the annual Halloween trip to the Half Moon Bay Pumpkin Festival. With a charming small-town parade, excellent food (including the best pumpkin pie in the world), and great entertainment, the Half Moon Bay Pumpkin Festival is the best way for a family to enjoy a fall afternoon.

One of the best parts of the festival is a special children's area complete with games, face painting and a special stage for kid-oriented entertainers. The many displays by the Bay Area's leading artists and crafts designers are also a great way to get a head start on Christmas shopping.

There really is something for everybody in the family to enjoy.

Submitted by Edward Mooney

for all ages

5. My name is Nicholas, and I'm 6 years old. I just went to a real neat place in Berkeley, and it's close to my home in El Cerrito. You'll love this place if you want a slight climb (on steps), and a cool view of San Francisco Bay and the three bridges (Bay, Golden Gate, and San Rafael).

Visit Indian Rock at Indian Rock Park in North Berkeley. Just take Indian Rock Avenue (off Arlington Circle) for one block and you are there. You can also walk from The Alameda and Solano Avenue up Indian Rock path to the park.

Submitted by Nicholas Henry - Age 6

6. For almost twenty years, four close friends, "The Classy Chassis," Sue Gaver, Doris Miller, Gertrude McGaha, and Ruth Polanchek, have celebrated their birthdays together.

We have dined in the finest of restaurants all throughout Northern California. One of our favorite outings is a trip on the historic "Spirit of Sacramento" for brunch. The paddlewheel riverboat departs from Old Sacramento. It has three completely enclosed, climate-controlled decks for dining and entertainment.

There are lunch and dinner cruises; but our favorite is the Captain's Brunch, which features gourmet food and champagne during a two-hour cruise on the Sacramento River.

Submitted by Doris Miller

7. Each year our little group of three to four couples selects a weekday in December to travel to San Francisco.

We begin with an early Christmas breakfast, drive to the city, park where we can leave the car for about 12 hours, and begin. Our starting point is usually the department stores: Emporium with the huge tree and wonderful train setup on the top floor; Macy's with its wonderful Christmas floral decorations; and Nieman-Marcus with the tasty food samples on the top floor.

Then we move on to the hotels -- the Fairmont, Mark Hopkins, St. Francis and Hyatt Regency, which at times have choirs to add to the spirit. At the Hyatt Regency, you can find a wonderful seating area in the lobby for a nice hot drink and perfect view of the ice skating rink and its skaters. Finally, the Financial District. Here, we go into all the bank lobbies, which are just beautiful. You may even find a train or Santa display.

Now, it's time for dinner. Each year we choose a different restaurant where we "ooh" and "aah" over our viewings of the day and rest our feet. This is a special day that starts the holiday season for us.

Submitted by Judy Kuechler

8. When my mother grabs my leash and says to me, "Do you wanna go to Point Isabel?" my tail uncontrollably rotates in circles. Sometimes the drive seems endless ... are we there yet ... are we there yet?

Then when we turn off Highway 580 onto Central Avenue in Richmond and head for the San Francisco Bay, the salt-water smells blowing in the window, and I know this is about as close to Heaven as you can get. No, I'm wrong. Heaven is when she unsnaps my leash and I can run free. There are important things for me to do: chase bird shadows and investigate mole holes.

I share this beautiful space with surfers, children flying kites, strollers, runners, lots of wagging tails and smiling faces.

This beautiful park is located right on the Bay. It has rolling hills, wind-swept cypress trees, open spaces and wide pathways. The sweeping view is an ever-changing drama. The park is partially fenced, has picnic tables, water and restrooms.

*Submitted by April
(and Anne Rifenrath)*

9. My favorite thing to do in Northern California is hard to choose because there are so many things available. I like playing baseball, swimming, football, basketball and hockey. I also like Golfland and Chuckie Cheese.

When I'm not playing, I like going to professional sports games like the 49ers, A's, Giants and the Warriors. And when I can't get to a 49ers game, I listen to KGO Radio because it broadcasts the games.

Submitted by Jimmy Panetta - Age 7

10. One of Northern California's most fascinating attractions is the Salinas International Air Show. Every year we get to experience the awesome power of military jets, from here and abroad, ripping through the sky creating sound waves that pound on your chest as the afterburners bolt across the horizon.

The air show is one of the few opportunities civilians have to get a close look at the scientific wonder of the machines that fought in Desert Storm.

There are displays and tours with plenty of armed forces' personnel to answer questions. We've seen Russia's MIG 29s perform, and we saw the Canadian Snow Birds do stunts that were death-defying.

We particularly enjoy the show because it's held in the wide-open space of the Salinas International Airport. Although there are a lot of people, it never feels crowded.

Submitted by Jaime & Jennifer De Anda

5. Nicholas visits Indian Rock Park. 6. Sue, Doris, Gertrude and Ruth, "The Classy Chassis" pose for the camera before brunch. 7. A Christmas breakfast with Judy and her traveling companions. 8. April at her favorite park. 9. Jimmy smiles before playing football. 10. Jaime DeAnda at the Salinas International Air Show.

11. *The Renaissance era.* 12. *Chris and family get ready for a little boating at Lake Camachi.* 13. *Members Blancha Burden and Evelyn Martin during "Victorian Days In the Park."* 14. *Erin and her friends having fun at the beach.* 15. *Eurkea's Christmas Parade.*

11. Renaissance Faires are sprouting up all over California, not to mention all over the country. My wife, Diane, daughter, Emily (she's 4 years old), and I travel all over California, from San Luis Obispo to Lake Tahoe, reliving the glory and splendor of the Renaissance and Queen Elizabeth I. We have organized a Scottish household in the Pittsburg area and once a month, from March to November, we donn kilts and bodices (not to mention corsets -- ouch!) and travel back in time to the 16th century.

We live as the Scottish Highlanders would have lived when they traveled. Sleeping in tents, with our wool to keep us warm. Eating what we cook over an open flame.

Rising at dawn, we start our activities and prepare for the coming day. The fire is started to warm the water. The women start to prepare the midday meal, or start spinning the freshly combed wool. Behind them can be heard the clash of swordplay, men and boys learning the finer points ... so to speak. Prepare the way for the chief and her ladyship as they approach! Clear the way and ensure that there is warm broth to help take the chill off their bones. The clatter of dice can be heard, as can curse words spoken over the card game. Interrupting the chief's draught, he is forced to intercede in the ensuing argument. The gammers are quickly silenced. Soon the morning march begins. It is expected that the Scots show a display of their power. The men fall into ranks with claymore, ax, and sword held high, the early morning sun reflecting off the silver blades. As the drums and bagpipes start to slice through the relative quite of the morning, the English would surely know the Scots are in town.

A harsh and brutal time, yet simple and unpretentious. A time when people had everything they needed, and needed only those things they had ... mostly family.

Submitted by Richard Hills

12. My name is Chris Boyd. I went camping with my family, grandmother, aunts, and uncles. I learned how to ski. We also went hiking and swimming at a great place called Lake Comanche.

Submitted by Chris Boyd - Age 15

13. Do you know the history of South San Francisco? Why is the sign, "South San Francisco -- The Industrial City," declared a landmark? As part of San Bruno Mountain, the sign is a guideline for pilots to use when coming into San Francisco International Airport on foggy and rainy days, as well as a guideline for motorists on Highway 101 that will direct

them to San Francisco.

The South San Francisco Historical Society invites everyone to attend its public meetings, where local citizens give their history of the city. The public is also invited to attend the society's annual banquet in October, when awards are given to an outstanding citizen.

Located at Magnolia Center, 601 Grand Ave. Admission is free.

Submitted by Evelyn Martin

14. My sister, brother, cousins, mom, dad, and I all love to go to Capitola Beach. Every Fourth of July we stay for seven days and nights at my grandma's house.

During the day we build sand castles, dig big holes for sandcrabs, and bury each other in the sand. We all love to play in the ocean together. We also go up the river on paddleboats. Five people can go at one time. The owner makes us all wear life preservers in case we fall off the boat.

We take walks on the wharf and see people fishing. This year I want to learn

how to fish, too.

At night, we have a barbecue, and then we roast marshmallows and make s'mores (graham-cracker sandwiches with marshmallows and Hershey's chocolate bars).

Submitted by Erin Downey - Age 7

15. Most people go to Humboldt Coast for the big trees and the rocky coastline. We went to see the nighttime-truckers Christmas convoy.

One hundred big rigs all dressed up for Christmas. It was a spectacular display of hundreds of flashing lights, reindeer, Santas in their sleighs, snowmen, merry-go-rounds, Christmas trees, and much more.

We all lined up to watch the show in front of the Historic Tudor-style Eureka Inn. It was packed with party-goers dancing to live bands, and people having dinner and cocktails.

There are lots of things to do and see in Eureka. Take a carriage ride through Old Town, go to Fort Humboldt State Historic Park, or visit the Maritime Museum.

Submitted by Jo Ann Casso

16. My favorite thing to do in Northern California is practically in my back yard. We live about 10 minutes from the Larkspur Ferry Terminal, which is also a 45-minute cruise from San Francisco. A beautiful ferry boat takes us past the verdant Larkspur shores, Angel Island, stunning views of the bridges spanning San Francisco Bay, Alcatraz, and finally we arrive at the shore. The sea air is marvelous, and gets us ready for the long walk to North Beach, or to Pier 39, or to Chinatown, or to Fisherman's Wharf. Whichever stop we choose, we reward ourselves with a delicious lunch.

After lunch we return to the Ferry Building, stopping en route for a cappuccino or a latte before boarding the boat for another delightful 45-minute cruise back to Larkspur. This trip is a great way to have a mini-cruise, walk for exercise, and dine in a different part of the city, all in just a few short hours.

If you ever get the urge to take a world cruise, you can always take the Larkspur Ferry and dream a little -- it's surprising how many fellow dreamers you will meet on this run.

Submitted by Mary Ruggiero

17. I like to do a lot of things. But my favorite time of the year is the Christmas season. I like to visit Santa Claus at his home. I tell him what I want for Christmas. Sometimes, he gets it for me.

Submitted by Johnny Panetta - Age 6

18. One of my favorite places in Northern California is the Western Railway Museum in Suisun City. It operates on weekends and holidays. It is a way to relive the slower pace of life that was pre-1950's vintage.

I was just growing up when the "Roar of the Four" street-car tracks on Market Street were beginning to disappear. The old Market Street railway lines, bought by the San Francisco Muni Railway in 1944, began disappearing also.

There was a former Key system train that ran on the lower deck of the San Francisco-Oakland Bay Bridge. Before 1958, you could travel from San Francisco to Oakland to Berkeley and back to San Francisco by train.

The Western Railway Museum is a unique way to relive history.

Submitted by Al Hall

16. Mary boards this beautiful ferry boat for a cruise from Larkspur to San Francisco. 17. Johnny patiently waits for Santa Claus. 18. Former San Francisco "Iron Master" street car which ran on the K, L and M lines.

19. I like to attend the monthly meetings of a group called UFOCUS, which meets in Concord. Usually, there are several speakers covering different topics on UFOs, or unidentified flying objects.

Topics might be about the results of a recent photo analysis, or the progress someone is making on a case, or hot, breaking news, or a representative from a support group for people who have been abducted by aliens.

The group does not hold a particular position. Anyone who speaks (and everyone is allowed about fifteen minutes) can expect respectful questioning from the audience.

Submitted by Budo Calvin

20. When it was hot in Hyampom Valley in the summertime, we packed a picnic lunch and rode horses up South Fork Mountain, always with a coat or sweater. My slogan was: "Better to have it and not need it, than to need it and not have it," because the mountaintop could be cold.

After the road was built, we went in the car. This is the only mountain in the whole world, I am told, that doesn't come to a peak, but is more like a ridge that runs for 70 miles or so. We would go berry-picking for wild raspberries, called black caps, to make pies

early in the summer. Then in the fall we went on the mountain and picked Elderberries to make jelly.

It is a nice place to spend the day or camp. It is seven miles to the top. I never walked to the top, but I knew people who did. That was when there were only trails.

I came to Hyampom Valley on Dec. 10, 1927. The South Fork of the Trinity River and Hayfork Creek come together in the middle of Hyampom Valley. That's why the mountain is called South Fork Mountain.

Submitted by Edith M. Garrett, 86 years young

21. On a beautiful day for a picnic, we call our friends, pack the basket (maybe stop at KFC), and off we go across the Richmond Bridge. We go through west San Rafael, past picturesque countryside, redwood trees, and ferns to Samuel P. Taylor Park.

After a while, we go on to Olema, where we get out to stretch our legs and browse in flower and gift shops. Then we continue west to Inverness, skirting Bodega Bay, a picturesque European-type town. A short drive beyond Marshall, we arrive at Tomales State Park. We find a secluded picnic table overlooking the beautiful string of beaches on Tomales Bay.

We enjoy our picnic, then follow a trail for a short walk, enjoying the different types of fauna. Mid-afternoon, we pack up and head for home, via Highway 1 south, past Stinson Beach and marvelous views of the Pacific.

We arrive home in the late afternoon, delightfully refreshed after less than a 100-mile drive.

Submitted by Virginia M. Kelley

20. Right: Edith (sitting to the left) in a recent family photo.
21. Below: The Kelley's enjoying a feast at Tomales Bay State Park.

TOP THINGS TO DO

WINDSURFING 1

This is the sport for young and old alike. It is as low-impact or as high-impact as you wish. If you are a water person, you'll love it.

This sport requires time to learn and can be frustrating in the beginning. However, it feels great to overcome the steps and go on. Also, there's the fear factor, such as sailing under the Golden Gate Bridge for the first time. A great memory.

Our favorite spot is in Rio Vista. From early April to late November, it's the place to be because of the steady winds and the opportunity for beginners and advanced sailors alike. It's great. Also, there is a shallow beach for children to play.

The people that come are friendly and helpful to beginners. It's a place where you can sail all day, have a good barbecue dinner, do some fishing after dark, and wake up to another day of sailing.

Submitted by
Peter & Lisa Pennington

AIR FORCE MUSEUMS 2

One of my favorite things to do is visit the various Air Force Museums in the state. Each have aircraft on display and museums with displays on the mission of the base, base histories, and other aspects of the Air Force experience. Here is a list of bases I like:

Beale Air Force Base in Marysville, which was the home of the SR-71 Blackbird, and is now home for the U 2s.

Travis Air Force Base in Fairfield, which has a F-100, F-102, F-103, F-104, F-105, and F-106 on display.

McClellan Aviation Museum in North Highland. It has a C-47, EC-121 Constellation, MiG 17, and about 15 other airplanes on display.

At Edwards AFB in the Mojave Desert, there is a visitors center at NASA Dryden Flight Research Center. If you want to see where the right stuff is, Edwards Air Force Base has tours.

Submitted by Timothy McIntosh

RC PLANES 3

My favorite recreation is to fly my model airplane in Coyote Hills Park, which is located just north of the Dumbarton Bridge. The flat surface of the bay generates a smooth air current, so when the breeze hits the hills it must rise. That rising air makes it possible to keep my glider in the air. Although the northern-most hill is the highest, we like to use the second hill because there are fewer rocks and more places to land.

My son, Adrian, is eager to help me before the flight. We check the controls for the last time, the batteries are charged. Then we face the wind, and there she goes. On a clear day we can see the high-rises of San Francisco and San Jose.

Just south are the three transmitter towers for KGO Radio. To the north is California State University at Hayward.

Some Sundays you can find eight or more planes in the air. We are all members of the Academy of Model Aeronautics.

Submitted by Artur Hernadi

BEALE AFB 2

1 **WINDSURFING**

3 **RC PLANES**

4 SALTY LADY

Salmon sportfishing aboard the spacious, fast, 56-foot "Salty Lady," with Capt. Roger Thomas at the helm, is the most enjoyable getaway in Northern California.

Not only is it relaxing, but I caught four salmon in one day, and this is not a fish story. Anyway, it all translates into being able to share two salmon with other folks who didn't catch the limit, and having a grand backyard barbecue with friends - still another great experience.

Needless to say, this was only the beginning of ongoing, delightful times on the "Salty Lady" fishing trips. It's a great place to meet people from all over the world, or old-time San Francisco fishermen. You hear lots of fish stories, breathe healthy fresh air, and also see whales and other sea life that Roger points out along the way.

I have told many people about this great outing. It's a chance to get a free dinner, if you are lucky, from your own back yard: the ocean.

Submitted by Mary Vanicik

5 WALKING LADIES

There is a walking group in the Bay Area that knows no limits. Its fearless leader, Tom Filcich of Mill Valley, takes them where they want to go and brings them back alive. He does this with different groups, four days a week. I've been with the Thursday group for two years, and I have found an extended family.

A recent trip to Albany Hill, and to the Bay marshlands near the racetrack, showed me how congenial this family has become. We struggled up the hill, hiked to the marshlands, and found time for play. The hill was a challenge, and we encouraged each other. On the way to the marshlands, a starting gate parked outside the racetrack provided the toy for playing. With my camera always by my side, it was a grand photo opportunity.

Walking in the San Francisco Bay Area is a rich experience. Covering the grounds to your destination with a walking group has many rewards. There is so much to see, plenty of friends to talk with, and the pleasure of reaching your goal. Mine is to see more of the Bay Area, enjoy being outdoors, keep walking, and have an extended family of friends.

Submitted by Lavon Nelson-Sutherland

6 BIKING LADY

One of the best ways to experience the natural beauty of the Monterey Peninsula is by bicycle. There are many enjoyable bicycling routes throughout the county, and bicycle rentals are available in several bike shops.

Perhaps the most spectacular bike trail in the entire United States is the Waterfront Recreation Trail. It runs from Pacific Grove to Seaside, with the most popular section being the easy, mile-long stretch between Fisherman's Wharf and Cannery Row. The 18-mile trail also passes by such notable landmarks as the Point Pinos Lighthouse, Lover's Point in Pacific Grove, The Aquarium, Monterey's Window on the Bay waterfront park, and Del Monte Beach. The variety of stops along the route range from viewing otters frolicking in the surf just yards away, to brilliantly colored kayaks, to a host of cappuccino shops, bakeries and restaurants.

The Waterfront Trail is also an extraordinary place to take a stroll, rent a surrey, or strap on some rollerblades. The scenic trail is flat and paved for much of the way, making it easy to accommodate the very young, strollers or wheelchairs.

Submitted by Karen Allison

4 SALTY LADY

6 BIKING LADY

BALLOONS ABOVE 7

We got up at 5 a.m. to be at Windsor by 6 a.m. It was worth it. We enjoyed champagne and strawberries while we waited. Finally, they were ready, and one by one the air brought them alive and into the sky.

It was cool and clear. What a sight! Color filled the sky. Each one with its own personality. There were at least 25 balloons trying to outdo each other. What a sight to enjoy.

The oohs and aahs from the crowd. Which balloon was the best? It was not easy to pick just one. We surely enjoyed the morning.

Until next year ...

Submitted by Lauretta Chipley

8 PLAY GOLF

We love to play golf. We'll go anywhere, anytime to try a golf course or to play a favorite. It is important to us that we do not ride a golf cart. We walk.

A favorite trip for us will be to start fairly early in the day, and have a leisurely breakfast on the way to our 11:30 a.m. tee time at the Pajaro Golf Club in Watsonville.

After our round, we drive to Pacific Grove for the evening, and play that wonderfully fun course the next day. The front nine is the city course, the back nine the seaside course.

There are very nice places to stay, and great places to eat. The golf courses in this area are just marvelous, and Pacific Grove is our favorite. The people who run the golf course are friendly and make us feel welcome.

*Submitted by
Paul & Virginia Allen*

9 SAILING

Sailing on San Francisco Bay is as good as sailing gets. San Francisco is widely regarded by sailors worldwide as one of the best sailing spots on earth. Many international sailing regattas are held on the Bay every year. With harbors, marinas, sailing schools and safety courses offered around the Bay, the opportunities for boating experiences are limitless.

Boating in the San Francisco area is not limited to the Bay. You can go "out the bridge," as we call going under the Golden Gate Bridge, to go salmon fishing or whale-watching or pleasure boating.

An evening of boating on the Bay is an unforgettable experience. The lights of San Francisco are framed on both sides by two of the world's most famous and beautiful bridges. The distinct sound of the foghorn ends your evening.

We can be spotted sailing our 38-foot ketch, MIST, on the Bay.

Submitted by Magnus N. Akerblom

TRAINS 10

Mountain air and diesel locomotives. What a combination. Nothing else is like a trip to the railroad museum in Portola. It offers caboose trips around the museum's loop of track. On any summer weekend you can see and ride behind engines from the original generation of diesel locomotives.

Western Pacific Railroad lives at the museum, which was started to save equipment and memories from the Western Pacific Railroad. It was lucky to get diesel engines and freight cars from Western Pacific after its merger with the Union Pacific Railroad.

The Portola Railroad Museum also has a special program called Rent-a-Locomotive. Portola is about an hour north of Reno and Truckee.

Submitted by Peter Parrish

8 PLAY GOLF

Photo: Verne Paule

7 BALLOONS ABOVE

9 SAILING

Photo: Verne Paule

10 OLD TRAINS

MOTORHOMING 11

I would like to tell you about a special place to camp, with an RV or just for a picnic. Lake Francis Resort is located a half-hour east of Marysville in the town of Dobbins. The resort is nestled next to Lake Francis, which includes fishing, swimming and row-boating.

The campground is filled with 100-foot pines, oaks and madrone trees. The campground area boasts 100 RV sites, most with full hookups, romantic cabins and plenty of tent camping.

Lake Francis Resort also has a large clubhouse that is replicated to look like an old western town. Truly quaint. Real antiques hang throughout the restaurant, the saloon and the general store. There's also a video arcade and banquet hall.

There is sand volleyball, softball, horseshoes, shuffleboard, and, get this, plans for a driving range and putting green.

The resort is halfway between Bullard's Bar and Collins Lake. And it's only a short, beautiful drive to historic Nevada City.

Submitted by Patricia L. Lopez

KAYAKING 12

On Father's Day this year, we were looking for a fun thing to do to escape the 100-degree weather in the Santa Clara Valley. My husband suggested kayaking in Monterey Bay. Never having done this, I pictured myself locked into the kayak upside down in the water. But we had seen other people in the bay enjoying the sport when we had lunch on the wharf there.

My husband, myself, and our two teen-agers went to a sport shop and rented two single kayaks for the kids and one double for my husband and me.

We first stopped close to the kelp beds and watched the otters. Some mother otters wrapped their babies in kelp. Then we paddled over to the sea lions and watched them bask in the sun. We meandered through the boats in the harbor and ended up on the beach.

We were gone about two hours, but it was very enjoyable. I would recommend going in the morning when the water is calm. Overall, it was a fun and exciting day out on the bay.

Submitted by Joanne Bratcher

BACKPACKING 13

My favorite place and favorite activity in California is backpacking along the John Muir Trail.

The Muir Trail passes through what many backpackers agree is the finest mountain scenery in the United States. Some hikers may give first prize to some other place, but none will deny the great attractiveness of the High Sierra.

This is a land of 13,000 and 14,000 foot peaks, soaring granite cliffs, lakes literally by the thousands and canyons 5,000 feet deep. It is land where man's trails touch only a tiny part of the whole area, so that by leaving the trail you can find utter solitude.

It is a land uncrossed by roads for 160 airline miles from Walker Pass to Tuolumne Meadows. And, perhaps best of all, it is a land blessed with the mildest, sunniest climate of any major mountain range in the world. Though rain does fall in the summer, it seldom lasts for more than an hour or two and then the sun is out, shining for most above the horizon.

Submitted by Thomas Winnett

KAYAKING 12

11 MOTORHOMING

13 BACKPACKING

14 HIKING TRAILS MAINTAINED

My favorite leisure-time activity involves work, but also a lot of exercise and satisfaction. I organize a monthly trail crew to build and maintain the hiking trails in Castle Rock State Park.

The park is located in the Santa Cruz Mountains above Saratoga, and is approximately 3,600 acres. It is kept in a semi-wilderness condition.

No vehicles are allowed except in designated parking areas. Our support comes from youth groups, families and many individuals.

Our rewards are the thanks we get from visitors hiking the park.

Submitted by Anthony Beere

15 MALIBU GRAND PRIX

If you and your family are looking for a place to go, there is a great spot for all ages and personalities. It's Malibu Grand Prix in Redwood City.

Malibu Grand Prix has everything you'd ever want in a fun center. For the sports personalities, you could either play baseball or miniature golf. There is a very large and fun baseball batting cage where you can rent a helmet and bat. There is also a miniature golf course (my personal favorite) that is very, very big. The holes are original, and if you make a hole-in-one on the 18th hole, you get a free game.

There is also a huge arcade area in the main building with games anywhere from Ghostbusters to Terminator 2. Anyone who is a fan of video games or pinball will love this section of Malibu. There is also a small restaurant.

Whatever your pleasure, you'll love Malibu Grand Prix, because it's the best fun center ever.

Submitted by Erin McCormick

SKIING AND MORE... 16

My favorite leisure activity is a combination of water and snow skiing. The Lake Tahoe area is the premiere location for these events. During May or June, if there's enough snow, I like to snow ski in the morning and water ski in the afternoon.

After all of the skiing is done, I relax with an inner tube ride behind a boat. For anybody who has not been fortunate enough to enjoy this back-breaking activity, I will explain it briefly. An inner tube is tied to a ski rope, which is attached to the boat. You climb onto the inner tube and hold on tight. When you are ready, signal the boat with a thumbs-up. As the boat pulls you along, your goal is to hold onto the tube. The boat's goal is to find as many waves as possible, because each wave represents an airborne event for the tuber. Tubing not only builds self-confidence, but it also reinforces your will to live.

Submitted by Daniel Spinozzi

MALIBU RACEWAY 15

Photo: Faye Dandy

14 **HIKING TRAILS**

16 SHIING

Photo: Verne Paule

Index
(Alphabetical)

AA Ranch, *40*
Allen, Rosie, *10*
Allied Arts Guild, *57*
Antelope Lake, *42*
Aptos Beach, *86*
Asilomar Beach, *48*
Auberge du Soleil, *13,31*
Avenue of the Giants, *74,77*
Barnes & Noble Bookstores, *2,6,52*
BART, *53*
Baxter, Ted, *11*
Beachcomber Inn, *32*
Beale AFB, *100*
Bell Glen Resort, *91*
Beltane Ranch, *65*
Benbow Inn, *33*
Benecia, *53*
Beringer Winery, *31*
Berkeley, *52,53,93*
Big Brothers/Big Sisters, *2,5,81,82*
Big Sur, *50,75,82*
Bjorklund, Chris, *65*
Bodega Bay, *28,93,99*
Bodega Bay Lodge, *28*
Botanic Garden, *52*
Brava Terrace Restaurant, *67*
Bridgeport, *47*
Bristow, Jon, *77*
Bucks Lake, *42*
Burford, Stan, *66*
Burns, Gene, *73*

Burnt Ranch, *38*
California Old Faithful, *30*
Calistoga, *63,67,73*
Campbell, Tori, *68*
Capitola, *69,97*
Carmel, *49,50,69,70,72,84*
Caruso's, *56*
Castle Rock State Park, *108*
Chateau Hotel, *30*
Chateau Mt. Helena, *71*
Children's Hospital (Stanford), *57*
China Beach, *55*
Chinatown, *98*
Christian Brothers Winery, *15*
Ciolino, Leo, *62*
Clarke, Chris, *14*
Cloverdale, *22*
Collins Lake, *106*
Copeland, Brian, *13*
Country Rose Inn, *82,90*
Coyote Hills Park, *100*
Cypress Inn, *69*
Davis, Pat, *18*
De San Juan Garden, *51*
Del Norte County, *74,78*
Dillon Beach, *84*
Downienville, *34*
Dunbar, Jim, *8*
Dumbarton Bridge, *100*
Eason Jim, *17*
Edmonds, Greg, *16*
Edwards AFB, *100*
El Verano, *29*

Empire Mine, *36,37*
Enrico's, *60*
Eureka, *33*
Fairmont, *94*
Feather River Canyon, *42*
Ferndale, *33*
Ferrin, Lynn, *79*
Fioli, *56*
Fisherman's Wharf, *49,102*
Ford House, *22*
Fort Bragg, *93*
Fox's Lakeside Restaraunt, *19*
French Laundry, *64*
Gaige House Inn, *29*
Garden in the City, *59*
Gate House Inn, *90*
Geist, Mary Ellen, *75*
Gilroy, *90*
Gilroy Visitor's Bureau, *60*
Glen Ellen, *28,65*
Gold Quartz B&B, *91*
Golden Gate Bridge, *55,80,81,100,104*
Golden Gate Bridge Park, *59*
Grass Valley, *19,35,36,37*
Greggains, Joanie, *76*
Guerneville, *17,76*
Half Dome, *78,79*
Half Moon Bay, *67,68*
Hamilton, John, *2*
Healdsburg, *27*
Hennessey, *64*
Heritage House, *9,23*
Hill House, *24*
Hodges, Allison, *80*
Hotel Leger, *34*
Humboldt Coast, *97*

Hunt, Ken, *71*
Hyampom Valley, *99*
Indian Head Beach, *20*
Jack London Square, *4,52*
Jack London State Park, *29,30*
Jackson, *19,34,46,90*
Jamestown, *37*
Jenner, *76*
Jimenez, Lynn, *15*
Jimmy Lowe's, *71*
John Muir Trail, *79,106*
Johnson Farm, *58*
Kelley House Museum, *22*
Kennedy, Susan, 63
Kincaid's Restaraunt, *4*
Klamath Basin, *38*
Klamath National Forest, *43*
Lake Almanor, *19*
Lake Comanche, *97*
Lake Delvalle, *13*
Lake Francis Resort, *106*
Lake Merritt, *53*
Lake Shasta, *39*
Lake Tahoe, *70,80,96,108*
Larkspur Ferry, *98*
Lassen Park, *41,43*
Laub, Bryna, *72*
Little River, *23*
Little River Inn, *12,18*
Little Switzerland, *29*
Livermore, *13*
Luckoff, Michael, *70*
MacKerricker Beach, *86*
Malibu Grand Prix, *108*
Manchester Beach, *85*
McArthur-Burney Falls, *41*

Memorial Park, 56
Mendocino, 8,12,18,22,24,25,26,
    27,63,73,93
Mendocino Hotel, 22,24
Meyers, Michaelynn, 67
Mill Valley, 71,102
Mission Ranch, 50,82
Mission San Juan Bautista, 51
Moaning Cavern, 36
Mono County, 47
Monterey, 48,49,50,67,69,72,102,106
Montgomery Woods, 25
Morton's Warm Springs Resort, 28
Mt. Lassen, 40
Mount St. Helena, 30
Mt. Shasta, 7,39,41,42,43
Mt. Tamalpais, 16,74
Muir Beach, 74
Napa, 11,13,15,30,31,64,70,71,73
Nevada City, 19,35,36,37
Nix Shann, 71
Nob Hill, 58
North Beach, 98
Oakland, 52,53
Oakland Museum, 53
Obester Winery, 26
Occidental, 33
Opus One Winery, 13
Orick Beach, 32
Owens, Ronn, 13
Pacific Grove, 48,49,104
Pacifica, 67
Pajaro Golf Course, 104
Pebble Beach Lodge, 84
Pelican Lake, 55
Perruman, RJ, 74

Pescadero, 56
Pinnacle Beach, 86
Pismo Beach, 84
Point Arena, 27
Point Reyes, 14,20,54
Poimiroo, John, 78
Praire Creek State Park, 32
Presidio, 81
Queen Inn, 35
Red Bluff, 41
Redding, 38
Redwood City, 108
Redwood Forest Ranch, 22
Redwood National Park, 32,77,78
Reid, Karen, 80
Renaissance Faire, 96
Richmond Bridge, 99
Rio Vista, 99
Ritz-Carlton Hotel, 58
Rusco, Gene, 69
Russian River, 7,17,27,80,76
Ruth, 40
Sacramento, 32,18,41,85,94
Sailing, 104
Salinas, 95
Salty Lady, 56,102
San Francisco, 11,26,59,60,70,76,
    80,94,97,98,104
San Francisco Zoo, 60
San Juan Bautista, 51
San Martin, 90
San Pablo Dam, 92
Santa Clara Valley Koi &
Water Club, 57
Santa Cruz, 11,48,57,67,69,86
Saratoga, 69

Sausalito, 55,56
Sea Ranch, 17,26
Seacliff Beach, 86
Sebastiani Vineyards, 8
Shell Beach, 84
Shelter Cove, 32,84,85
Shumann, Mike, 12
Silver Lake, 44
Silverado Country Club, 31
Siskiyou, 43
Sonora, 34
Sonoma, 8,15,17,27,28,29,30,71,73,80
Sorenson Resort, 45
Stagecoach Hill, 33
Starkey, Joe, 9
Stinson Beach, 14,54,99
Suisun City, 98
Sulfur Works, 42
Sutter Creek, 91
Terra, 70,73
Tilden Park, 52
Tomales Bay, 20,85
Tor House, 49
Tra Vigne, 31
Travis AFB, 100
Trees of Mystery, 31
Trinity Alps, 63
Tule Lake, 38
Walcoff, Rich, 20
Wappo, 73
Ward, Bernie, 71
Watsonville, 104
Wattenburg, Bill, 19
Western Azalea, 33
Western Pacific Railroad, 104
Western Railroad Museum, 98

Wilder Ranch, 57
Wilson, Pete (Gov.), 78
Windsor, 104
Windsurfing, 99
Wolf House, 29
Wygant, Ted, 8
Yosemite, 7,45,77,78,79,81
Yountville, 30
Yuba River, 35
Zephyr Cove, 80

CALENDAR OF EVENTS

GILROY

June 16 • Father's Day Antique Fair
Monterey Street shuts down to give pedestrians the opportunity to browse for antiques and collectibles from over 100 antique vendors. Musical entertainment, face painting and great food make for a great day. *Free admission. 408.842.6436.*

July 4 • 4th of July Celebration
Fireworks show is held after dark over Christmas Hill Park sponsored by the City of Gilroy. *Free to the public. 408.848.0460.*

July 19 • Gilroy Garlic Festival Golf Tournament
This is the kick-off event for the Garlic Festival held at the Gilroy Golf Course, Hecker Pass Highway. *408.842.1625*

July 20 • Gilroy Garlic Squeeze Barn Dance
Kick-up your heels and dance to country western and rock & roll bands. Held at Christopher Ranch, 305 Bloomfield Ave. Tickets must be purchased in advance. *408.842.1625*

July 26, 27 & 28 • Gilroy Garlic Festival
The 17th Annual Gilroy Garlic Festival. A gastronomical affair, featuring garlic foods, wine, arts & crafts and continuous entertainment. Held at Christmas Hill Park. Friday gates open at 9 am to 6 pm, Saturday and Sunday 9 am to 5 pm. *408.842.1625*

August 17 & 18 • Antique Street Fair and Brewfest
The streets of Gilroy will be transformed into a mini-village of micro-breweries. Tasting, antiques, music and more. *Free admission. 408.842.6436.*

SACRAMENTO

April 28 • Festival De La Familia
Open-air market with foods, crafts & music from 25 Latino countries. Old Sacramento & Downtown Plaza; *916.552.5252 category 4127.*

May 24-27 • Sacramento Jazz Jubilee
Internationally renowned festival featuring more than 100 bands from around the world; *916.372.5277.*

June 1 • Sacramento Children's Festival
Hands-on educational & art activities, storytelling, pony rides, entertainment. Old Sacramento & Downtown Plaza; *916.552.7971.*

May 23-September 26 • Thursday Night Market
Street performers, crafts, farmers market, musical entertainment, food booths. 5pm-10pm, K Street, between 7th and 13th Streets. *916.442.8575.*

June 14-16 • California Railroad Festival
Exhibits & activities for children & families, handcar rides, toy and model railroad exhibits. California State Railroad Museum, Old Sacramento; *916.552.5252 category 7245.*

July 3-7 • Folsom Championship Rodeo
PRCA sanctioned event, nightly fireworks, Dan Russell Arena, Folsom; *916.985.2698.*

August 10-11 • Japanese Cultural Bazaar
Ethnic food, cultural shows, demonstrations, games. Buddhist Church, 2401 Riverside Blvd.; *916.446.0121.*

August 16-September 2 • California State Fair
Exhibits, food, top name entertainment, carnival rides, nightly fireworks. Cal Expo, Business 80 & Exposition Blvd. *916.263.3000.*

August 30-September 1 • Greek Food Festival
Ethnic food, entertainment, marketplace. Sacramento Convention Center Exhibit Hall, 13th & J Streets; *916.443.2033.*

Come enjoy the Jazz Jubilee – May 24-27.

An cook-out during the Garlic Festival.

Photo: Tom Myers